All American Christmas

All American Christmas

Rachel Campos-Duffy
and Sean Duffy

HarperCollins books may be purchased for educational, business, or sales promotional use. For information, please email the Special Markets Department at SPsales@harpercollins.com.

Imprint and logo are trademarks of Fox News Network LLC.

FIRST EDITION

Endpaper illustration by Doloves/AdobeStock, Inc.

Unless credited on the Illustration Credits page, all other images © stock.adobe.com and Shutterstock, Inc.

Insert art courtesy of mika48/Adobe Stock Images and FourLeafLover/Shutterstock, Inc.

Library of Congress Cataloging-in-Publication Data has been applied for.

ISBN 978-0-06-304664-1

21 22 23 24 25 LSC 10 9 8 7 6 5 4 3 2 1

Contents

All American Christmas

Introduction

Rachel: For Christians around the world, Christmas is one of the most important religious holidays of the liturgical year. That's a pretty obvious statement, but in our secular culture it's easy to forget that Jesus is the reason for the season. While devout Christians struggle to keep the spiritual meaning of Christmas alive and central in our culture, they also embrace the fact that everyone, including non-practicing Christians and non-Christians, loves Christmas!

I love how much my non-Christian friends looked forward to Christmas. Not believing in Jesus never deterred them from buying and trimming trees and decorating their homes. Indeed, our more secular traditions, such as cookie exchanges and watching *Rudolph the Red-Nosed Reindeer*, do something similar to what those fundamental beliefs in Christianity do; they unite us through common practices while also pointing out that we come from different backgrounds and celebrate the holiday in unique ways. It's also so American! E pluribus unum. Out of many, one. One family's way of doing things isn't better or worse; it's just different. And adding other people's traditions to our own is part of the evolving joy of Christmas.

Marriage, especially interracial marriage, is another way Christmas traditions evolve and meld into something new and beautiful. For us, that meant bringing Irish and Spanish/Mexican Christmas and Catholic traditions together.

Sean and I don't just come from different ethnic backgrounds, we also come from different parts of the United States, which presents some interesting regional (and weather!) differences too. Growing up in northern Wisconsin, Sean would tell you that no self-respecting family would have a fake tree.

Sean: When we got married, the very first tradition Rachel embraced from my family was a live, freshly cut Christmas tree. Rachel's Mexican-American dad is from the land of saguaro cactuses in the Arizona desert. Her mom grew up in a big city, Madrid, the capital of Spain. On top of that, Rachel was a military brat who lived most of her life overseas, so growing up, artificial trees were all she knew.

Rachel: I remember being so amazed that we could just drive a couple miles into the woods, pick out a tree, and take it home. Now, every year, not long after Thanksgiving, we set a date, load up Sean's chain saw, and go together as a family to cut down our Christmas tree. We blast Christmas music in the SUV and argue the whole way about what tree species we should pick this year.

Sean: Shortly after Rachel and I were married I had a Christmas tree mishap. Let's just say our fresh blue spruce looked like the Leaning Tower of Pisa. That's when my dad stepped in with a great piece of manly Wisconsin advice. His advice wasn't about the birds and the bees. It was about the trees. Specifically, tree stands. "Sean," he told me, "you get what you pay for, and size matters. Get a big stand with a wide base and you'll never have a problem."

And you know what? He was right! Ever since I got a big tree stand, we've never had an issue with a Christmas tree leaning or falling again.

Rachel: Over the years we learned to adapt and adopt our Christmas traditions and, in some cases (mincemeat pie comes to mind), drop certain ones altogether. Settling on what traditions fit your particular family and lifestyle is just part of the process, and every family has the same trial-and-error journey in establishing traditions that are worth continuing.

Sean and I share a real passion for Christmas and we fully embrace the whole holiday season from Advent (the four weeks leading up to Christmas) all the way through to Epiphany, or Three Kings' Day, which is on January 6, when we celebrate and open gifts again. On January 5, our children put their shoes under our family altar table in the living room. Instead of leaving cookies and milk like they did for Santa, they fill their shoes with sugar for the camels. In the morning, the Three Wise Men have left each of them three gifts, just as they brought the baby Jesus three gifts—frankincense, gold, and myrrh.

In this book, our FOX Family members share stories that will delight you, surprise you, make you laugh, and sometimes cry, but more than anything else, they will virtually welcome you into their homes, their past, and their presents—in both senses of the word! They share stories of their secular traditions as well as the role that religion plays in their lives and celebrations of the Savior's birth.

It should come as no surprise that as journalists, they are wonderful storytellers, so we've included these stories in their own words. And they didn't just supply us with exciting and memorable stories.

Inside this book you'll find tantalizing recipes from the wonderful

All-American Chex Mix (thanks, Dana, for her sister Angie's take on this one!) to Sandra Smith's Scandinavian Krumkake.

We've also included play lists and mentions of our FOX Family members favorite holiday tunes. Whether it's a secular classic like "The Twelve Days of Christmas" or the joyful hymn "Hark the Herald Angels Sing," or a few less familiar that you're going to want to check out for yourself—they make up a grab bag of good listening.

No matter what part of the country our FOX Family and Friends were born in or now live, or from what part of the world some of their traditions originate, whether they were an only child or one of a large brood, the members of our extended FOX Family had a few things in common—Christmas was a time of year they all associated with family, food, fun, and childhood memories that brought joy into their lives.

You're about to learn a bit about the gifts we loved, the songs we sang, the decorations we hung, the church services we attended, and the people and places that mattered most to us on Christmas.

As you put another log on the fire, curl up with a warm blanket, and settle in for a midwinter's read, we thought we'd kick things off by sharing with you how our FOX Family and Friends get into the spirit of giving. There are no ghosts who will visit upon you, but we will be reliving some of our favorite moments with you. We wish you all a merry Christmas wherever you are and however you celebrate this most blessed and joyous holiday.

The
Joy of
Giving

Dana Perino

*Dana Perino remembers working Christmases at the
White House and childhood holidays on the Wyoming range.
Giving, she explains, is what the season is all about.*

I was born in Wyoming, but my parents moved us to the Denver area when I was two years old. That didn't mean we entirely left the ranch life that my grandparents and my parents' siblings were still living. My dad went to work for Western Farm Bureau Life Insurance, and because of where and how he was raised, he knew a lot about insurance and about farm or ranch life. My uncle Matt still runs a ranch up in northeast Wyoming, in the Black Hills. For nearly every vacation, including summers off from school, we'd drive up out of Denver and head north into ranch land that spread for hundreds and hundreds of miles.

Dana and Jasper getting into the Christmas spirit.

We'd get up into, literally and figuratively, Marlboro country. The advertising company did a few photo shoots on my grandpa's ranch. They used my grandpa's quarter horses in the shots, and my uncles could be seen in their yellow rain gear. The men being featured in the photos could ride and rope, so it wasn't just about being rugged and handsome. There was hard, physical labor to be done. "They were good cowboys," my grandpa said.

It's high desert terrain in that part of the US. So, with few trees and weather fronts coming down out of the mountains, those Christmas trips were most often windy and cold. I didn't mind the conditions, though. The weather could be harsh, but I have very fond memories of being with extended family. My favorite Christmases as a kid were spent at the ranch, being with my cousins and my aunts and uncles. And even though it was Christmas, the livestock still needed tending to. At Christmas, it was most often Uncle Matt who had to excuse himself from the festivities for a bit to get chores done. I don't ever remember him complaining about it. That was what ranching was all about. Some people romanticize the life, but it's a lot of hard work and sacrifice. So if I had to go to the White House or work during the holidays while sitting in a warm office, it sure was more comfortable than work the ranchers did.

That said, during my childhood Christmases we still found time for fun. I didn't have to do many chores on the ranch, but the one thing I did that I really loved was occasionally having to bottle-feed a calf whose mother had abandoned it. Calving season didn't coincide with Christmas, but being able to feed those adorable calves would have been the best Christmas gift ever. I still remember going down into the basement to mix the powdered formula with water in a big steel sink. We'd fill the bottles, secure the nipple, and then hold on for dear life as those hungry calves went after the milk. It was a "chore," but it was delightful.

In addition to all the wind, that part of Wyoming got a fair amount—that's the master-of-understatement Wyoming way of speaking that means "a lot"—of snow. (Or, if the winds were howling, you'd hear somebody say, "It's blowing a bit.")

One year a fair amount of snow and winds blowing a bit combined to produce a blizzard that lasted for days. That Christmas trip, we spent most of our time indoors. The wood-burning stove had a real appetite, and we fed it and were rewarded with warmth that kept the cold and wind outside at bay. They were howling, but hardly anyone ventured outside to give them a chance to get in. We spent most of our time in the main rooms of the house, packed in tight at a table playing cards. I didn't think of this then, but in a lot of ways it was a scene out of a TV show or a movie. We joked and laughed and ate well. At night we settled into bed beneath a pile of blankets and quilts and afghans.

With all that snow, one of the favorite things we kids could do was go sledding and tobogganing. These were the old-fashioned wooden types. We would get dressed up in our bulky snowsuits, tuck hand-knit scarves around our necks and faces, and tromp out in our moon boots to a nearby barn. Parked outside of it was a pickup truck that Grandpa had loaded with our sleds and toboggans. We'd pile in with him, or a few of us would ride in another pickup with my dad and his brother—there would eventually be seven grandkids total—for the short drive to a nearby hill.

Grandpa had four-wheel drive, so he was able to take us up to the top of that hill. We'd get out, and then one of my uncles would get himself seated at the front of the toboggan. We needed an adult's weight at the front in order to get the most speed. The rest of us would clamber onto it, putting our feet in the lap of the person ahead of us, forming a kind of oversize double helix. Someone would give the rider at the rear of the toboggan a push in the back to get us started, and soon we were holding on for dear life. We would fly down that hill once we'd gotten a groove worn into the snow. Grandpa would have driven back down the hill so that we could load up the truck and get driven up again. I can still feel my face tingling from the cold and hear our excited voices over the sound of the defroster in the truck's cab trying to keep up with all our breathing.

We'd be getting cold, but of course we wanted "one more time." At some point Grandpa would pick up the CB radio to tell my grandmother that we were finished and heading back in. Not that she needed reminding, but he'd add that she should get the hot chocolate ready. Later, holding that mug and breathing in its steam did the trick of warming us up.

And, of course, there would be cookies to eat. Grandma was the best, most precise baker and decorator of cookies in the county. She was a legend. Of course she used cookie cutters to get all the right shapes. I can still picture the Santa Claus figures and how she would put these hard silver balls of sugar on the end of his hat. The same with all the snowmen and the Christmas trees; every bit of them was just so.

Angie's Famous Chex Mix Recipe

3 cups each Corn Chex, Wheat Chex, and Rice Chex
1 cup lightly salted cashews
1 cup lightly salted almonds
1 cup Dot's Homestyle Pretzels
¾ cup (1½ sticks) unsalted butter
¼ cup Worcestershire sauce
1 tablespoon Lawry's Seasoned Salt
1½ teaspoons garlic powder
1 teaspoon onion powder
Few dashes of Slap Ya Mama cajun seasoning

1. Preheat the oven to 250°F.

2. In a large bowl, mix cereals, nuts, and pretzels together; set aside.

3. In an ungreased large roasting pan, melt the butter in the oven. Stir in the seasonings. Gradually stir in the cereal mixture until evenly coated.

4. Bake 1 hour, stirring every 15 minutes.

5. Spread the mixture on paper towels to cool, about 15 minutes.

6. Store in an airtight container.

Cranberry Nut Biscotti

½ cup (1 stick) butter, softened
1 cup sugar
2 large eggs
1 teaspoon vanilla
2 teaspoons orange zest
2½ cups flour
2 teaspoons baking powder
¼ teaspoon salt (if butter was unsalted)
1 cup chopped pecans or walnuts
1 cup chopped dried cranberries

1. Preheat the oven to 325°F.

2. Cream together the butter, sugar, eggs, vanilla, and zest in a heavy-duty mixer. In a medium bowl, mix the dry ingredients with the nuts and cranberries, then add to the mixer. The mixture is very stiff and may need to be finished by hand.

3. Line 1 or 2 large cookie sheets with parchment paper and form 4 logs from the dough. Flatten down the logs until they are approximately 2 inches wide. Bake for 35 minutes, rotating the sheets and switching positions halfway through. Remove the sheets from the oven and reduce the heat to 300°F. Let the logs cool for 15 minutes or until cool enough to handle.

4. Cut each log on the diagonal into slices and place the biscotti slices upright on the cookie sheets. Bake an additional 30 minutes. Cool completely before packaging.

As you can probably tell, Grandpa wasn't the typical grizzled, tough-as-nails rancher—at least when it came to his grandkids. He could have easily made us trudge up that sledding hill instead of driving us. He was a kindhearted man. Around the property, trees often got blown over by the wind or were cut down for firewood. What was left, the small branches and small trunks, went into a pile. Those less usable pieces were called "slash." At some point, they'd need to be burned in a huge bonfire. Except Grandpa often didn't want to do that. Over time, rabbits would build their dens among those branches. He didn't want to burn up their homes.

So I guess you can see how work and play figured into my childhood Christmas memories. I don't know if you can truly call this a Charles Dickens *Christmas Carol* moment, but in 2008, when I was President George W. Bush's press secretary, we were burning the midnight oil quite a bit. The president was dealing with putting together a relief package for those suffering from the housing crisis and other issues. I noticed that in our office, my staff was engaging in more whispered conversations than usual. They seemed agitated. I was wondering what was going on, and I knew it wasn't enough to wonder; I had to get an answer. I called a staffer into my office and got what I was looking for. We were so busy that none of us had had a chance to go Christmas shopping. So I said, "Okay, here's what we'll do." With help from the staffers, we devised a schedule that allowed each of them a day off to shop. We'd cover for whoever was absent that day and make sure they didn't come back to a huge overload of work.

Sure, it was a small sacrifice, but we weren't the only ones who did that kind of thing for others. President Bush always stayed in Washington, DC, for Christmas Day. He'd go to Camp David instead of Crawford, Texas, so that his staff and the Secret Service detail assigned to him and the family could have Christmas with their families.

Sometimes what we thought would be a bit of White House Christmas fun turned into more stress and work than was intended. My best friend, Jeanie

Mamo, was in charge of Barney Cam. Post-9/11 the number of White House visitors who could come to view the Christmas decorations was severely restricted. So Jeanie came up with the idea of putting a camera on the First Dog, Barney, and having him walk through the house giving a tour. Mrs. Bush loved the idea so much that we repeated it every year. Barney had his own mind, and often his idea of what the tour should consist of didn't fully match Jeanie and her staff's ideas. Still, the Barney Cam brought a lot of people joy, so in the end, whatever work and frustration it may have caused was worth it.

This past year, of course, it wasn't work that kept me away from my mom at Christmas. Like it did for so many families, COVID-19 put a damper on the holiday. My mom refused to let that difficult reality interfere too much and extinguish our holiday spirit. My mom is a very talented pianist, and she has always loved to play Christmas carols. This year, because we couldn't be together in person, she made a video for me and for my younger sister. It was of her at the piano playing all our favorite songs.

I loved hearing her play, and the music brought back memories of Christmas when I was a kid and at home in Colorado. I do remember getting a boom box as a present, and given the time when I got it, I'm pretty sure I popped in a Michael Jackson cassette to listen to. I was also reminded of sitting with my younger sister and watching *A Charlie Brown Christmas*, and then of course *Rudolph the Red-Nosed Reindeer* and *Frosty the Snowman*. I never really liked *How the Grinch Stole Christmas*, but my sister loved it so much. I was too young to be considered a grinch, but we have photographic evidence that I was a wannabe tree toppler. I was so fascinated by the ornaments that I would grab them. To ensure the tree's safety, and mine, my parents placed the tree inside the playpen.

Those TV specials usually came on after the Christmas catalogs had arrived and we each had a chance to leaf through them for ideas for our wish list. I pored over the JCPenney and Sears catalogs. I stopped to consider my choices and lingered over the descriptions. Finally I'd circle the items I wanted to add to my list. One year, I found out about a Santa hotline we could call to speak to him and speed up the process of getting our lists into the right hands. I begged and p-l-e-a-s-e-d and bugged my mom and dad until they okayed the call, which cost several dollars. I was, to put it mildly, very happy about that.

One of the best gifts I ever got was a play kitchen, complete with an oven, pots, and pans. I already had the imagination I needed to cook up delicious meals for all my dolls and stuffed-animal friends. I also had a *Sesame Street* playhouse that would unfold, and I was right there with Big Bird and all the other residents hanging out on the steps of the best neighborhood in the world. It was amazing to live on a block where I could have so many friends.

I am, still today, a list-making machine, and those toys must have been among what I'd asked for. I don't recall any really extravagant gifts or wishes, and things like getting Bonne Bell lip balm in my stocking made me very happy. Maybe that was because of all the wind and cold in Wyoming! We also got foil-wrapped chocolates and candy canes in there, and they were a real treat.

Of course, I also love giving gifts, and when I was working on *The Five*, we did a Secret Santa gift exchange. The best gift I ever gave during that period was for Jesse Watters. A segment of the show was called "Facebook Friday," and someone asked us via Facebook what was one gift we really wanted at Christmas that we never received. Jesse mentioned that he'd wanted a red leather Michael Jackson jacket. I had drawn Jesse's name and was joking that I would get that jacket for him. My producer Mina Pertesis managed to track one down. We gave it to Jesse, and he still says to this day that it was one of the best Christmas gifts he ever received. It's a great feeling when you give the right gift to the right person. The mix of surprise and delight when a gift connects with someone is worth all the time and thought that goes into it. Gift shopping never seems like work. Recently we've been giving gifts of wine with labels that say "Jasper Wine." The labels feature a picture of our dog, a vizsla named Jasper, and seeing him on there brings a smile to our faces and to the recipients' faces also.

The message of giving is what the season is really all about. My family went to a Lutheran church, and my sister and I were part of the bell choir that played Christmas hymns. I always associate those bells with the true sound of the season. My parents were also part of the congregation that helped resettle Russian refugees who were fleeing the Soviet Union to find a better life here in the United States. My parents and others would sponsor these families and assist them with everyday things. Whether it was helping the families settle in their homes or apartments, assisting them in navigating the public transportation system, or aiding them in dozens of other ways, they demonstrated how important it was to be of service to others. Sometimes it was as simple a gesture as us driving to one of the Russian families' homes to drop off Christmas cookies. They didn't have to be as perfect as the ones that Grandma made. Baking them and delivering them didn't feel like work at all. It was just what you did because it was the right thing, a good thing, a nice thing to do for others. Maybe that's the secret to the season. When you're with family and when you're doing things for family, it never feels like you're making an effort. It's never work; it's joy.

Dana Perino is the cohost of *America's Newsroom* (weekdays 9–11 a.m. ET) and *The Five* (weekdays 5–6 p.m. ET).

Jesse Watters

*Battle-hardened War on Christmas veteran Jesse Watters has learned
a few things during holidays past: among them, that stuff really doesn't
matter all that much, but gifts are a great way to show you care.*

My younger sister, Aliza, and I grew up in the 1980s. This was the era when Oliver Stone directed the movie *Wall Street*, and Michael Douglas's character used the phrase "Greed is good." It was also when President Ronald Reagan was in office, and there was this mood of go-go capitalism all around. My parents, pardon the pun, didn't buy into all of that. They didn't buy into the idea that making a lot of money and spending it on lavish gifts was the best way to instill values in their kids' lives. So while they were generous and we got our fair share of nice gifts like bicycles, skateboards, and toys,

Young Jesse before he became a foot soldier in the War on Christmas.

they taught us valuable lessons about having modest expectations and not putting such a big emphasis on material things.

Just about the time that all the Christmas television specials were coming on and my wish list was growing, my mom would sense what was going on in my mind. "Now, Jesse, this is going to be a thin Christmas," she'd tell me. She didn't want me to be too disappointed if, when my sister and I woke up on Christmas, we ended up with just a few gifts under the tree. Looking back now, I understand the lessons my parents were trying to teach. I never held any animosity about not getting everything I wanted. I can see now that my parents did the best they could within their means. My mother was the lower-school admissions director and writing instructor at William Penn Charter School while my father served as the middle-school principal there. Later, when we moved to Long Island, they held similar positions. So, like most educators, they weren't earning a huge amount of money. But they were doing their best to teach us and make us aware of what really mattered in life.

Apparently, one of those lessons involved dental hygiene. My sister and I still tease our parents about some of the stocking stuffers we got. In our house, tradition had it that we opened our stockings before any of our gifts. At the bottom of the stocking, we'd find a couple of pieces of fruit, apples or oranges, and then there would be a toothbrush, toothpaste, and sometimes dental floss and one of those plastic containers of Tic Tacs. I sometimes wondered if they were trying to let me know that I had a problem with bad breath. I also realized that those bottom-of-the-stocking "presents" were likely things they'd saved from our trips to the dentist. You always walked out of that office with a little goody bag of things, and my mom—at least I think it was her idea—saved those freebies and regifted them.

I don't think the salad tongs and other unusual gifts for children came courtesy of the dentist. Among the other gifts I got, and you have to keep in mind that both of my parents majored in English, were books. I remember getting lots of books. Some of them were new, but again, frugality and regifting came into play. Quite a few of the books were older, clearly used, copies. Some of them had seen better days. They had cracked and split spines, the cloth or leather covers were fraying at the edges, and pages were dog-eared and coffee stained. Many of them must have come from my grandfather's library. With some regifted items, I don't think I knew that they weren't originally intended for me, but every now and then I'd open something, and it would say, "To Anne and Stephen: Merry Christmas!"

As I said, we laugh about these things now, and it's clear to me that my parents had their hearts and minds in the right place. All the emphasis on material things that came to dominate Christmas, what was going on in the culture that promoted the importance of wealth, needed to be tempered somehow. And the truth is, with one exception, I was really pretty content with receiving a football as a gift. I didn't need the latest, greatest techno item or things like that.

That one exception, the thing my parents never were able to get for me, my version of Ralphie from the movie *A Christmas Story* wanting a Red Ryder BB gun, was a Michael Jackson leather jacket. As a child, I idolized Michael Jackson. I not only idolized him; I wanted to be him. One of the non-regifted gifts I got was a cassette tape of his amazing album *Thriller*, which came out in 1982. All I wanted for Christmas was that Michael Jackson leather jacket, the one that had thirty zippers. So, here I was, this little white kid growing up in Philadelphia, hoping and hoping that come Christmas morning, I'd be dashing through the snow in my new leather jacket. I was seven. I had no idea how expensive and impractical—I would have grown out of it in no time—that jacket would be. But you know how it is when you're a kid—you absolutely convince yourself that because you want something so badly, there is no way you're not going to get it.

That Christmas morning, after we went through our stockings, we opened presents. I looked at one box and thought, "That's the one!" I opened it, and sure enough, it was the one. I lifted it up—and it was a decorate-it-yourself sparkle-glitter Michael Jackson glove kit. Later I applied the glue that came with it, sprinkled the glitter, and was pretty content with at least having that part of my idol's signature look.

Fast-forward a number of years, and I'd just started working at FOX's show *The Five*. Dana Perino found out about my Michael Jackson obsession and, as part of our Secret Santa gift exchange, got me that jacket. It was worth the wait! Nothing could "beat it." I still have it, and it's great to think about how thoughtful a gesture that was.

It's funny to think of my Michael Jackson fascination in this context. My paternal grandfather would join my family on Christmas Eve. During cocktail hour, I would come into the living room dressed in a blazer, gray flannel pants, and a button-down shirt. I'd stand in the middle of the room with all eyes on me. I'd raise my flute to my lips and begin to play. Talk about pressure! I'd started lessons in the fourth grade and stopped taking them in the eleventh grade. Each year during that span, I'd have to put on that demonstration of my growing talent by playing a few Irish jigs, a couple of Christmas carols, and whatever else was in my repertoire. So, along with my increasing anticipation of gifts and family get-togethers and time off from school, Christmas meant extra time rehearsing for that at-home performance.

Maybe I should have spent more time practicing for the Penn Charter School's Christmas Concert. I can't recall what year it was, but I jumped in either too soon or too late for the flute part that was in the song's chorus. After the concert was over, my family had to acknowledge the elephant in the room. "That was rough." Nothing like it ever happened again during a performance. I had given it my best, and it was a learning experience.

My mom was very much of a Christmas traditionalist and very community spirited. You put those two things together, and I have memories of us going door-to-door in our neighborhood in Philadelphia to sing Christmas carols. My parents would insist that my sister and I put on turtlenecks and wear our blue blazers. Along with a few neighbors and friends, we'd tour the streets. We'd knock on a door, and as soon as it was opened, we'd burst into song. I don't think I knew this at the time, but I believe that some of the enthusiasm and energy was fueled by liquids that came from hidden flasks.

I do remember one other Christmas besides the bad musicianship one, when I was worried that things might not go as well as I hoped. I must have been a typical teen or preteen, moody and at the mercy of my changing biochemistry. When I asked my mother what she wanted for Christmas, she said, "Respect." I thought, "Okay. If it's respect you want, then that's what you're going to get." I went to the computer, chose a font, increased the size of the type to as large as would fit on a piece of paper, and typed "R-E-S-P-E-C-T." I printed that out, tore off the edges of the dot matrix printer paper, and framed it.

When my mother opened my gift, I sat and waited anxiously for her reaction. She smiled. She beamed. She held it up to show everyone. She was genuinely

A gift Jesse's mom didn't see coming . . .

quite pleased, and she has held on to it all these years, and I still respect her, and love her, for all that she has done for me and all the ways she put up with me back then. I wish I could say that she had the same positive response to my giving her a foot massager one year and a set of dish towels another. I think she detected a lack of foresight and heartfelt emotion behind those two. Fortunately, I am a better gift giver today, and despite the lessons my parents taught me about materialism, I have to confess that I do believe that nice, thoughtful, big, and sometimes expensive gifts are important, that they do mean something to other people, and that they are a reflection of how much you love and think of others.

I admit that I spoil my twin daughters a bit. I love being able to bring them into the city to see the tree at Rockefeller Center. They're still young enough that a trip to FAO Schwarz is a real treat for them. I'm fortunate that the kids-at-Christmas scenario is going to stretch out for the foreseeable future. My wife, Emma, and I welcomed a child in the first part of 2021, and that's exciting.

Christmas is my favorite holiday, so for as many years as possible on Christmas Eve we're going to get cozy as a family and watch *Home Alone* together and eat shrimp cocktail and have cake and eggnog. We'll wake up early, put on our robes, and go downstairs to sit around the tree and open presents. We'll spend the rest of the day in our pajamas, playing with toys. As a kid, for me there was nothing better than a white Christmas and going out sledding or having snowball fights. We live in the city now, and as convenient (and expensive) as it is to have venders selling Christmas trees on nearly every block, I do miss one aspect of what it was like when I was younger and we lived in Philly. We used to drive to the center of Pennsylvania, around Mechanicsburg, and go to huge tree farms with friends of my family and trek out with our boots and our hats and our saw. We'd just wander around acres and acres of the Christmas tree farm. And we'd find our tree, our special tree, and we'd get on our knees and saw it down. Then we'd lug it back, throw it in the bed of a truck or tie it to the top of the car, and then drive it all the way back to Philly.

One time after I'd moved away, my parents went to Pennsylvania and cut their tree down, drove it home to Long Island, and put it up. And then in the middle of the night, they heard this horrible sound downstairs, like there was a catfight, because my parents had cats. They went downstairs, and the cats were chasing a squirrel around the house. The squirrel had clung to the tree all the way from Pennsylvania to Long Island. When the tree was put through the netting device, the squirrel had been trapped in there and it was scared to death. It rode all that way, and then my parents put the tree up. At night it felt safe enough in the dark to try to escape and ran into the cats and there was a huge fight. My parents had to open the door. The squirrel ran out the door and we had an illegal squirrel because it crossed the state border.

I'm sure the tree was a large one. Size matters in my family when it comes to tree selection—especially in my mother's mind. The bigger the tree, the better. She wants the SUV of trees. Maybe that's because she wants plenty of space to put all the ornaments. And the house can accommodate tall ones too, with its high ceilings. My mother loves the classic look of a Christmas tree and decorations in general. Red and green and silver balls draped all around. Many of the ornaments are family heirlooms and those mementos do exactly what they should do—they bring back memories.

It's important to remember that what we celebrate in December is Christmas, and we should be wishing one another "merry Christmas" and not "happy holidays." Early in my career, I often went out to report from the front lines on the War on Christmas. I remember some of the ridiculous attempts various groups made to deemphasize Christmas—not being able to call a Christmas tree a Christmas tree and substituting the word "holiday" in front of "tree," banning candy canes, not putting lights up in a town square due to concerns over global warming. I tried to get to the bottom of all those stories, and I wasn't caroling, but I did knock on a lot of doors. I wasn't fueled by anything in a flask; I was out there defending a holiday and the traditions that the vast majority of us celebrate and hold dear. Those memories tie us to our past—to our families, to our friends, to our neighbors, and to those whose gifts were eventually repackaged and presented to children who understood and appreciated the spirit of the season. I guess we all just want to be startin' somethin' come the end of the year. I prefer that thing be what we know and love as Christmas.

Jesse Watters is the host of *Watters' World* (Saturdays 8–9 p.m. ET) and the cohost of *The Five* (weekdays 5–6 p.m. ET).

Bret Baier

From Christmases spent in the hospital with his son Paul,
Bret Baier has learned the value of giving back.

When it comes to Christmas, one of the best things about it, at least for me, is the surprise element that comes with celebrating the holiday with family. That's especially true when it comes to gift giving. I try to get something for people that they want but aren't really expecting.

One of my favorite Christmas surprises was in 2020. For quite a few years, after I took over as the host of *Special Report* from Brit Hume in 2009, I've included my whole family in taping a Christmas message for our viewers. When the kids were really young, I remember my son Daniel crawling all over the anchor desk for one of the earliest ones. That was a little hectic. "Take twenty-four!" I

The Baier family delivering gifts at a children's hospital.

would yell as we gathered Daniel before he crashed to the floor. And it was more than a challenge to get the kids to say the message properly—which made for some great bloopers for the end-of-the-year party. As the kids have gotten older, they're more used to the process, and now they've got it down pat. But this past year, before COVID, I decided to do a little improvisation.

As we were taping the Christmas message, Santa and Mrs. Claus came into the studio. The cameras kept rolling and caught the look on my kids' faces when they saw Mr. and Mrs. Claus escorting a little puppy. The kids had been wanting a dog for a while, so Coco, the little goldendoodle, was our way of granting their wish. The kids were, obviously, surprised and really, really happy. "Shocked" might be a better way of putting it, at least initially. Their reaction was caught on tape, and we used that for our annual Christmas message. It got a lot of responses. We'd been telling the kids for a while, "No. A dog's just not right for us yet." Coco was right for them that day and ever since.

I'm not complaining, but I think I'm a pretty easy person to buy presents for. My love of golf is no surprise to anyone who knows me. I started playing the game as a little kid, so I frequently received golf-related things for Christmas.

When I was a child, for a number of years in a row, we traveled to Puerto Rico to spend Christmas there. My mom worked as a travel agent, so she was often able to find us great places to stay in San Juan. I played a lot of golf in Puerto Rico at Christmas, so instead of skating or sledding, I was out on the course. One year, I received a set of Chi Chi Rodriguez irons for Christmas. I opened that gift while in Puerto Rico and that was especially nice because Chi Chi is from Puerto Rico, and he is a very charismatic and charming guy. It was great to be able to take those clubs out and practice with them immediately. And when I made a putt, I would pull out my putter just like Chi Chi and make his swashbuckling move and then pull the putter back down by my side. I was an only child at that time, but I still had a blast. My little brother, Tim, would come years later, and then I would help make Christmas special for him.

So now, as an adult and a father, I've kind of made it easy for my kids to figure out what to buy me. Golf can get pretty expensive, so I usually get a new range finder or a dozen golf balls that they know I prefer.

On the other hand, with my wife things are a little bit trickier. She doesn't play golf, so there's no easy go-to gift area that we can all rely on. Amy is a giving and wonderful mother and wife—so it's important for me to find the right gift for her—but in all honesty she just wants time with our family together. The other thing is, unlike me, she doesn't really like surprises. So, to figure out something for her, I have to pay close attention, read between the lines, and work hard to get a sense of just what the right thing is for her. There's no surprise there, just a bit of hard work and attention to detail.

My younger son, Daniel, has told me, "Just tell her to go out and get what she wants. Then that could be the present." I have to admit, we've done that a few times too. It takes away some of the surprise and some of the Christmas magic. There's nothing like the Christmas-morning anticipation of seeing what gifts everyone got and the great feeling of knowing that you made someone happy.

Of course, not all surprises are pleasant ones.

I grew up Catholic, and one year I was serving as an altar boy for midnight mass. Because it was such a special remembrance of the birth of Christ, that service was more elaborate than most. Instead of there being just two altar boys, the parish priests organized a mass with a processional. About twenty of us altar boys walked ahead of the priest. We each carried a lit candle. The thing is, we wore the usual cassock and surplus over our street clothes. What wasn't typical about our altar boy garments was that the surplus had a hood that we wore to cover our heads.

That Christmas Eve service, the church was packed, and I remember holding my candle and the next thing I knew I was on the floor looking up at faces that gradually came into focus.

I'd been carrying the candle too close to my body. The heat and smoke from the candle's flame got trapped in my hood. I collapsed on the altar and was carried to the sacristy, the room off to the side where the priest and the altar boys prepared for the mass. It was there that I was revived. I imagine the scene was scary, watching a young boy collapse like that at midnight mass. But everyone was made aware that I was okay. The priest gave me some grief about my "performance," but my family really gave me a hard time once we were back home and into the next morning at Christmas. We had a good laugh about it, and it isn't the typical Christmas memory or the typical surprise you want to provide for your family and your faith community, but that's one Christmas memory we retained.

Dramatic collapses aside, the church services were special to me, and I really got into being up front and a part of the sacrament. Christmas is not really about giving gifts, of course. Going to church and honoring the day of the Savior's birth make it a very special time of year.

Our parish put on a Nativity reenactment outside, featuring live animals. I had never experienced anything like that before. I really enjoyed watching that part of the Christmas story being played out, and a few times when living in the Washington, DC, area, my wife and I have sought out services that included live actors and animals performing the gospel story of Jesus's birth. Something about seeing live actors and animals gives the Christmas story immediacy and impact. Jesus came to earth in human form and lived among us, and those words on the page are clear, but seeing the reenactment in person makes it much more real and especially great for kids to visualize.

Come to think of it, maybe my love of surprises goes back to those times when we went to Puerto Rico. When we came back to our house in New Jersey, we discovered a fully decorated tree and presents beneath it waiting for us. It was as if Santa had still come to our house even though we were away in San Juan. That went a long way toward me believing in Santa. Whether we did or didn't make the trip to Puerto Rico, we did do our own decorating at home as well. My mom liked to change things up, so we would have different themes, like one year having a bear-themed tree. She'd have to buy different ornaments all the time, so we ended up with quite a collection of them. I also remember spending a lot of time trying to find the source of the lights not functioning properly. That was one of my jobs for both the tree lights and the ones we strung outside the house. We did a decent amount of decorating—it wasn't a "*Christmas Vacation* with Chevy Chase" kind of thing, but it was always great to come home at night to that scene. Out of tradition, we'd keep the lights up until January 6, the feast of the Epiphany, when the Three Wise Men came to visit the baby Jesus.

In most ways, our Christmas celebrations, both when I was younger and now as a parent, are fairly typical. But in one particular way our Christmases have often been very different. I wish I could say that we are part of a very, very small group to experience this difference, but that's not the case, unfortunately.

Our older son, Paul, is now fourteen. Due to five congenital heart defects he's had since birth, Paul has had to have four open-heart surgeries, ten angioplasties, and a stomach surgery. As a result, he, and we, have spent a lot of hours in hospital rooms. Some of those times have been during the Christmas season.

But that's where our love of gift giving—and giving pleasant surprises—comes in. Because of those earliest Christmas-in-the-hospital experiences we had when Paul was very young, and because we believe it's important to remember folks going through a tough time, we instituted a tradition of bringing toys to the kids on the heart-and-lung ward of Children's National Hospital in Washington, DC. We've been doing that since Paul was a baby, and he and his younger brother, Daniel, who is ten, are a big part of that act of giving.

We want to show our gratitude for all the help our family has received and to show the kids how it's more important to give than to receive. The boys are really into this annual tradition. So are my coworkers at FOX and the FOX DC bureau. My assistant Katy posts a wish list of gifts along with the ages of the kids, and people are so remarkably generous that we end up with a truckload of toys to bring to the hospital. It's fun to see the look on my kids' faces and on the faces of the kids on the ward, along with the expressions of the doctors, nurses, and all the support staff there. Sometimes Paul wasn't able to help distribute the gifts as we pushed large rolling clothes baskets down the corridors. Instead, he was one of the kids in a hospital bed. But he would get into the hallway—still connected to tubes in recovery—and say "merry Christmas and happy holidays" to all who walked by.

The gratitude goes both ways. One year, when Paul was eight and in a good place with his health and between surgeries, he went room to room allowing kids to choose their present from the big rolling pile of toys. Paul met a young boy who was waiting on a heart transplant operation. He told Paul that he was feeling better than he had in a long time, and he added, "You're really cool for doing this. I want to be friends when I'm out of here and maybe swim in my pool together!" The boy got his heart transplant and did very well. Paul was touched by that exchange and he frequently shares this story when he's asked about being in and out of hospitals so much.

So when I think of the stories of Christmas, that is the best one I have, because it passes on the spirit of giving to another generation, and it also has the spirit of thankfulness and gratitude for the doctors and nurses at Children's National and for God for getting us through what has been a big challenge. Paul's heart was "fixed" with three different donated aortas—sewn by the surgeon into his heart to make it pump the right way. We often think about the three families that lost a son or daughter, enabling Paul to live because they decided to donate organs. It's sad to think of those families and the family of whoever donated that heart to Paul's friend, but what an amazing gift of life to be able to give in the despair of their loss. I'm sure they know that their spirit of giving has meant a better life for another person. Another boy or girl is alive at Children's National because of that gift. It's beyond words and it's the true meaning of Christmas to us.

I also remember traveling to visit US troops in the Middle East as part of a USO tour in 2003. I've been to Iraq twelve times and Afghanistan thirteen, and it's always a humbling experience to see what sacrifices our military and support personnel make in service to this great country. On that USO trip, I was there along with the then chairman of the Joint Chiefs of Staff, Richard Myers. We flew in his plane as we bounced from country to country, visiting the "Stans"—Uzbekistan, Kazakhstan, Afghanistan, and Pakistan. This was before the twenty-fifth of December, but the bases were already decorated for Christmas, a nice reminder and boost for the troops who were so far from home. Robin

Williams was on that tour. He was amazing. He was a fairly quiet man—I spoke with him a few times—but when he went onstage, he was all manic energy, improvising his way through very funny performances day after day. He really gave so much of himself each time out there. He would start a lot of the shows yelling, "Gooood morning, Baaagram," or whatever base he was on, playing on the words from his 1987 hit movie *Good Morning, Vietnam*. General Myers got up every time and said one thing: "We're here for one reason—to wish you a merry Christmas and happy holidays and to say thank you!" I have a lot of amazing memories of the people I met on those trips, both as part of the USO and covering stories overseas. I traveled to seventy-four countries over my time covering the Pentagon and the White House and some of them during the holiday season.

Our family is now nearly obsessive about sending out Christmas cards. We keep extensive mailing lists that change and alter and are added to every time we get a new card from someone who wasn't on the lists before. More important, we get a family photo taken, and shortly before Thanksgiving, before Turkey Day, our cards will arrive with the message, "Happy Thanksgiving and Merry Christmas. We give thanks for a healthy and happy year." I like the idea of linking the two holidays. They're both about being grateful, and sharing that message is important to us as a family.

I lost my father in the past year, so I'm especially grateful that we have a Christmas ornament he sent us for each of the last thirteen years. He had our names engraved on them, starting from the year Paul was born until my dad's passing. We also have a remembrance of part of my career spent in Washington, DC, as chief White House correspondent. I've collected the White House and congressional Christmas ornaments from each of the last twenty years. So our tree has that national and familial history as part of it. We also make it a point to visit not just the big National Christmas Tree in front of the White House but also the ones that represent each of the fifty states. We try to go to the White House to view how the First Lady has decorated and the particular theme she's chosen. You would think

Christmas decorations would be apolitical and nonpartisan, but unfortunately even that line is sometimes crossed by critics of one side or another.

It's important to remember to give back. This past Christmas was difficult for everyone given the pandemic. For us, it was tough with Paul undergoing a complicated and risky surgery at Christmastime. If I was heartened by one thing, it was that more and more people were aware of, and grateful for, the sacrifices that health-care workers make. It isn't just during COVID-19 either—we are enormously grateful to all the people who've cared for Paul over the years, and especially those who chose to share their time and themselves on Christmas Day. Taking care of other people, putting others before you and your interests, that's a huge blessing. That's what Christmas means. When you see people putting their own lives at risk to help save other people's lives, it's both humbling and not surprising. The worst of times often bring out the best in these dedicated and compassionate people. We've all got a lot to be grateful for. And that is always a good place to start a New Year!

Bret Baier is the anchor and executive editor of *Special Report with Bret Baier* (weeknights at 6–7 p.m. ET) and chief political anchor of the FOX News Channel.

Brit Hume

*Brit Hume remembers the joys of Christmas in Washington, DC,
in 1953 and reflects on how Christmas is the one season
when we spend more time than usual thinking about other
people and their needs and wishes instead of our own.*

Christmas remains for me *the* holiday. This goes back to my boyhood. Christmas was the big one, especially then. Birthdays were nice and Easter was sweet, but Christmas was the best moment of the year. Part of my enjoyment was one tradition that we haven't kept up at my house, and I miss it. We would bring in a Christmas tree and it would stand there in the house untrimmed on Christmas Eve. I would go to bed, struggle very much to fall asleep, and in the morning I'd come out and find that Santa had

Washington, DC, in the snow.

arrived. There in the living room this splendid tree was all trimmed and ready to go, complete with gifts beneath it. That was such a huge thrill for me; all my anticipation was realized in that one moment that truly said "Christmas is here!"

I'm not certain if my parents had that as a part of their Christmas celebrations when they were kids. I suspect that they did but I can't verify that fact. Today, I don't know how many people decorate their trees on Christmas Eve for presentation the next morning. Mostly I see trees going up right after, or shortly after, Thanksgiving. Another aspect of Christmas that I can't verify, though family lore says it's so, is that my mother's side of the family, which was to a great extent German, had among its members the person who brought the tradition of having a Christmas tree to the state of Virginia. Perhaps that trim-the-tree-on–Christmas Eve tradition began back then. As I say, despite being a journalist, that's one story that I haven't investigated fully.

As a kid I didn't invest much thought into that subject either. I loved waking up to that decorated tree, but, as a typical child, I was more interested in the gifts I was about to open. My appreciation for the joy of giving, and surprising and delighting other people in a manner similar to what I experienced in waking up on Christmas morning, didn't fully develop until I was older. When I was growing up, I had an eclectic set of wishes through the years. Sometimes those were the most trivial of items; sometimes they were major things. One year it was a bicycle. Today, it seems, every child has a bicycle, but back then you were a member of a somewhat small group if you had one.

I very nearly didn't get to become a member of that club. This was back in 1953 when my hopes were nearly dashed. That summer my family and I attended a Washington Senators baseball game. The team was quite terrible, but watching a major league baseball game was always an adventure. That day, a Washington Senators pitcher, Virginia-born right-hander Bob Porterfield, won his twentieth game of the season, joining the ranks of Senators greats like the storied Walter Johnson. I'd gone to the game with my parents and a friend, Sandy Hillyer. We got so caught up in the excitement of this historic achievement that, despite direct orders not to, we joined a group of fans who ran out onto the field to pat the winning pitcher on the back. When we got back to our seats, we discovered that my parents had gone. We knew where the car was parked, so we headed out. I can remember feeling a rising sense of panic as I ran, breathlessly panting, trying to catch up to my parents. I skidded to a stop and my father turned to me and said, "Remember that bicycle you wanted for Christmas?"

"Yes."

"Forget about it."

I was devastated. Fortunately, by Christmas morning I had been forgiven. I went into the living room. There sat a Rudge bicycle. This was an offshoot brand of the Raleigh Bicycle Company, which was the pinnacle of the cycling industry back then. I didn't care. I was thrilled. I don't recall just how cold it was that Christmas Day, but that afternoon, along with my friend Sandy, who had also received a bike, we rode down California Street in Washington, DC. Our knuckles were frozen, but we were the happiest kids alive and we shouted out, "Merry Christmas," to everyone we passed on the sidewalks.

I had that bike for many years. Prior to getting one of my own, my family would go to what we called the Speedway, the road and sidewalks around Hains Point, a park down by the river. We could rent bikes there, and that was a huge deal. Riding a bicycle of my own seemed an impossible dream.

I didn't always ask for such extravagances. Another year it was a flashlight, another an alarm clock, and another a somewhat bigger gift, a portable Motorola radio. The family had a radio we all listened to, and it was powered by vacuum tubes and not transistors, so it was in a large wooden case. This one was smaller but dense, and even with its handle, it strained against the logic of it being called "portable." I loved it. I could listen to the programs I wanted to hear—*Yours Truly, Johnny Dollar*, a detective drama, and *The Adventures of Ozzie and Harriet* and other comedies like that. Those programs fired my imagination, and even after television came along and my fad-skeptical family stood outside a TV store to see what all the hoopla was about, radio remained a fixture in our household.

When I was fourteen, I had my first girlfriend. I was attending an Episcopal boys' day school, and she attended the sister school to that institution. I was crazy about her, just crazy about her. That Christmas she gave me a wallet. Inside it, she'd tucked away a photo of herself. On the back of it she wrote, "To Brit with love. Be good and never change." I was a very private teen, as most are, and was worried about what my parents or my younger brother might think, so I'd gone behind a chair to open that gift and read that note. You would have thought that Jane Austen had written those beautiful sentiments I was so taken with them. Subsequently I realized that they were somewhat cliché.

Despite having my own radio as I did, I wasn't interested in the news. Only after I'd gotten married during my senior year at the University of Virginia, and out of an increasing sense of desperation that I had to have some career, I'd taken a job as a cub reporter at a now defunct newspaper in Hartford, Connecticut. I loved the work from day one, and the rest, you could say, is history.

I wasn't earning much at the start, but still, life as a young married couple was very, very enjoyable. I know that many plots of television situation comedies and stand-up comics' routines revolve around men hating to shop generally, and shopping for wives and girlfriends particularly. That revulsion or embarrassment or whatever motivates that stereotype was never part of Christmas shopping for my wife. I really enjoyed picking out and buying clothes for her. Now I get to think about what to buy for my granddaughters.

My family still gets together at Christmas. For years my brother and his family and mine spent it at our house in the Virginia countryside. Later my daughter, my son-in-law, and my granddaughters joined us there from suburban DC on Christmas Day. But after years in and around DC, my wife and I decided that we'd had enough of the heat and the traffic of summertime. We've got a house in the mountains east of Pittsburgh now. We rattle around inside this four-bedroom place. We chose it because it is ideally set up for guests. The family comes up there for Christmas, and we so look forward to it. My dear wife goes all out to make it look as festive as possible, like something out of a movie. Last year we all watched the Christmas classic *Holiday Inn*, the musical for which Irving Berlin wrote "White Christmas."

Please don't, for your own good, ask me to sing the Christmas classic from that movie. I'm fortunate that my speaking voice hasn't diminished much with age, but my singing voice is an instrument that most people would prefer had faded out entirely—both then and now. Just because I can't produce melodious sounds doesn't mean that I can't appreciate them. I also have some particularly fond memories of Christmas and church and music. When I was at St. Albans School in Washington, we had an annual Christmas pageant held in the cathedral. It was one of the traditions that was always observed. And there was a hymn called "Of the Father's Love Begotten" I remember so vividly. The choir procession started from a place on the lower level of the cathedral. Their voices singing that hymn reverberated throughout the cathedral and grew louder as they came up and onto the main aisle. Those echoing voices were so moving and the words so meaningful. I remember that scene and those sounds as clearly as anything I can from going to those Christmas pageants every year.

Just so you don't think I'm being overly self-deprecating about my inability to sing, I'll share another cathedral moment with you. At George H. W. Bush's funeral at the National Cathedral, I was once again seated in a crowded space. Having gone to school on those grounds, I was familiar with the liturgy and the hymns, so I sang them. At the conclusion of the service, the man seated in front of me turned around and said, "You should sing very softly." I wasn't greatly offended. I said, "All that scripture enjoins me to do is to make a joyful noise unto the Lord."

For years one of the White House Christmas parties was for journalists, and I often went with a family member. One year I especially remember I took my older granddaughter. We got a ride from the FOX bureau with the late Charles Krauthammer, who was nearly paralyzed from a long-ago diving accident and got around amazingly well. Charles could seem a distant, even forbidding figure to those who don't know him, but my granddaughter wasn't put off in the least. She was so taken with Charles that she didn't want to leave his side. At the party, she went with him everywhere, just standing quietly beside him.

I've spent a bit of time in this piece talking about gifts, and some people, a lot of people, lament the commercialization of Christmas. For all that, Christmas is the one season when we spend more time than usual thinking about other people and their needs and wishes instead of our own. One result is that we, as a people, make more charitable donations during that time than at any other point in the year. We think about friends we may not have been in frequent contact with. We may be in touch with a relative whom we've not heard from in a while. Some people decide that it's a good occasion to lay aside any upsets or differences. And even if it is just about thinking in an unselfish way about what we might be able to buy for someone that will delight him or her, then I believe that's a very healthy thing for us to do.

Maybe giving gifts serves as a means to offset those moments when our parents insisted that we get on the phone to thank our aunt or uncle who sent a sweater or a scarf that as kids we couldn't have cared less about and we barely managed to dredge up an ounce of genuine appreciation from the bottom of our gratitude barrel. Or maybe we want to replicate the generosity and timeliness of gifts we received like the ones I did from my father's brother, my uncle "Smoke," as he was nicknamed. I could always count on him. Once, he sent me a toy filling station that had opening garage doors and realistic-looking gas pumps. He understood the heart of a child.

Even though I could be a bit of a brat when it came time for thank-yous, I'd like to think that my spirited ride on the Christmas of 1953 on that Rudge bicycle was more the norm. Greeting all those other people as I did was my way of saying, "God bless us, every one!" I know that I've been truly blessed and wish the same to all, and to all a good night. I hope you wake up on Christmas Day to a fully decorated tree, presents that delight you, and genuine gratitude that makes those thank-you calls as easy as mine were to Uncle Smoke.

Brit Hume is a senior political analyst for FOX News Channel.

Lawrence Jones

For Lawrence Jones, Christmas is a good reminder of the
sacrifices made to make Christmas special, and of why
it's vital to always strive for the good things in life.

In my family, Christmas was the best time of year. No matter what had been going on during the previous twelve months with extended family members, that was always the time when, if need be, differences were set aside and everyone came together. That meant that Mama and Daddy did their best to make sure we enjoyed Christmas and its true meaning as well as getting a few fun things to enjoy.

In my immediate family, I'm the oldest of three kids, and we kicked off the season on Thanksgiving. After the Thanksgiving dinner had been eaten, we gath-

A young Lawrence Jones.

ered together and put up and decorated the Christmas tree. It was artificial, but the sense of togetherness wasn't. My mama had me when she was seventeen, so my parents were young parents, but there was always a traditional vibe to that night and to the rest of the Christmas holiday as well. My daddy really got into the typical Christmas-card scene even though I grew up in Garland, Texas. He'd get a fire going in the fireplace before tree trimming started, Mama would make hot chocolate, and bit by bit we'd get the tree up and decorated. Nat King Cole would be singing about chestnuts roasting, but instead of going for a sleigh ride, we'd all get in the car and drive the thirty or so minutes to see the decorations that homeowners had put up in and around Dallas.

One of our favorite spots was a wealthy area where Jerry Jones, the owner of the Dallas Cowboys, and a few of the players lived at the time. Highland Park had wide streets that wound through the impressive homes. Lights were strung up in the trees, they framed the houses, and various still-life or animated figures stood on the enormous lawns. We were somewhat impoverished, and going to Highland Park felt like we were in a dream world. Every weekend between Thanksgiving and Christmas, we'd drive to a different area to admire how other people had decorated their places. I guess I could have looked at those houses and been resentful that those people had something that we didn't. That wasn't what happened. Instead, the trip was aspirational. I would say to myself, "Someday I'm going to build a house like that." Those drives gave me a sense of what was possible if I worked hard at school and had a vision for my future. My daddy played into shaping that view of what I could achieve. Many times, even when I was in primary school, he'd have me rewrite my book reports, and he always urged us to read, read, read.

It's not like we didn't make our best efforts at home to have a great Christmas

season. My mama worked as a nanny for a time, and my daddy was a computer operator. They were both employed and worked hard. But raising three kids even on two salaries can be a challenge. That was especially true when, while I was in the eighth grade, Mama developed lupus and eventually had to go on disability. At that point, I assumed the cooking duties, including at Christmas. We were kind of a make-do family. By necessity and because of Mama's creative impulses, we made a lot of our Christmas ornaments and decorations by hand. In addition to becoming pretty good with the tools of the kitchen, I got comfortable using a glue gun early on in life.

We didn't decorate outside the house, but inside, my mama always wanted to make sure the house was festive. I can remember her buying us stockings that we decorated for ourselves, and we had a few store-bought or gifted ornaments that we added to with creations of our own. Using pinecones, Popsicle sticks, cotton balls, and other things we could forage from around the house, we would use our imaginations and our skills. Craft time was family time, and we'd all sit together making various things and talking and laughing. We weren't on our cell phones (we didn't have them) or watching TV—we were bonding, and those hours spent making decorations are among the best times I can remember from the holiday.

It's too bad that as we've gotten older, the extended family doesn't get together as much as we used to. Funerals and family reunions are about it, but back then, family would come in from Waco, a two-and-a-half-hour drive, and drop by our place to eat. I got used to preparing a big spread for as many as fifty people. We didn't all sit down together at once, but family was coming in and out of the house at different times. They'd make up a plate and often take a plate home as well. The cooking came easily to me. Even before Mama got sick, I'd be in the kitchen watching what she was doing. She cooked from various recipes, and I read them, made them once, and then added my own touches.

For a young guy like me, the trade-off my mama made—having me cook while she cleaned behind me in the kitchen—was well worth it. Even when I was eight or nine, I'd be in the kitchen helping her out with the cooking. That was my apprenticeship. Eventually I stopped following recipes. I like to ad-lib a bit—a pinch of this and that, cooking by taste and smell and intuition rather than instruction. Dirty pots would never pile up, and I could just focus on the cooking and making people happy.

Whether it was frying a turkey, preparing barbecue, or doing up the side dishes—what we all seemed to like the best—I was in my own little happy place in the kitchen. So with all those people, all the Christmas spirit and catching up on events in our collective lives, we would throw down. This spread was no small thing, and platters of mac and cheese, green beans, greens, sweet potato pie, pecan pie, and carrot cake were coming off the stove or out of the oven regularly throughout Christmas Day. Thankfully my mama was an expert coupon clipper. We were just getting by, and that big meal was something my mama and daddy wanted to do and had to be resourceful for in order to make it all happen. Being together as a large family was more than worth the time, effort, and money.

We're a very religious family, so going to church on Christmas Eve was an essential part of our celebration. Leading up to Christmas, we'd assist at the church, helping set up the manger scene and rehearsing for and performing in the Christmas play. I enjoyed the services on Christmas Eve, and we'd stay up until midnight after they were over. Then it was game time and we'd open our gifts!

The somewhat unusual thing is, we never believed in Santa. Daddy would say, "Look, life is hard enough. I have to work so hard and bust my butt to be able to get you-all Christmas gifts. You think I'm going to let somebody else, some mythical person, take credit for it? No. I bought this stuff. I worked hard to earn it." That was a good lesson, I can see, but it didn't always make all of us happy. Once, my brother got in trouble because he shared my daddy's views on Santa with a classmate.

We were fortunate that, for a time before my paternal grandfather died when I was in fifth grade, our grandparents spent Christmas with us. My maternal grandparents would come by the house, even though my grandfather often worked late on Christmas Eve. He was a disabled veteran and still he managed to work and to treat his grandkids well. I remember that once he got me a bicycle, which was a huge thrill. I'm not sure how he felt about the whole "Santa didn't buy it, I did" issue, but I knew that bike was from my grandparents, and I was really grateful for what they'd done.

Unlike my brother getting in hot water for spoiling the Santa story, I got in trouble once at Christmas because I was a little too overeager about a gift I was hoping to get from Mama and Daddy. My mama was not a fan of guns—toy guns, real guns—being in the house. She didn't like anything to do with violence. But growing up, I wanted to be a police officer, and what was a policeman without a gun? So I put a BB gun or a toy gun on my wish list, even though my mama was against them. It never hurts to ask, right? I figured out where my parents were hiding the presents and was thrilled when I saw a toy pistol among them. I looked at the package and noticed that there was no holster for it. I wasn't happy about that, but because I was used to our do-it-yourself approach, I figured that was a problem I could easily fix. Imagination + cardboard + razor knife + hot glue = holster.

On Christmas, just after the stroke of midnight, I opened my presents and, surprise, there was my pistol. I left the room, went into my bedroom, and came out with my holster. Bad move on my part. Mama and Daddy figured out pretty quickly that I'd been sneaking around finding the stashed presents. They didn't have to say much. I knew I had to fess up. My punishment fit the crime, I guess. For two months, when all the other kids were running around shooting at one another with Nerf guns and other toy weapons, mine was tucked away on a shelf somewhere (I knew better than to sneak it out) while I sat on the porch watching and wishing. If you want to be a policeman, you'd better be a law-abiding citizen yourself.

Mama and Daddy did the best they could within their means. My mama might find a laptop computer at a thrift shop. She'd bring the ancient thing home and

Daddy would get it up and running. It wouldn't be the newest or the best, but at least we'd have one.

Only later did I really understand what kind of financial strain my parents were under. Mama was receiving disability payments but not a whole lot, and that added to the strain. We always got shoes and clothes, things we needed, and a few fun things, but it wasn't very fun for my mama and daddy. They were doing everything they could to provide for us, but the stress of it was taking a toll on them. At Christmas they had to resort to buying less for me as the oldest and more for my younger brother and sister. Then, when my brother got a bit older, they trimmed the amount they spent on him. I can see now that as exciting as Christmas was for us, those sacrifices and worries made the season difficult for them. They wanted to do so much for us it sometimes hurt.

One of the real pleasures for me now, as an adult, is that I can spoil my parents as a way to thank them for everything they did for me. I wouldn't be where I am in life if it wasn't for all they sacrificed and worried about. The funny thing is, "spoiling" them isn't as extravagant as that might sound. My daddy is happy with an Amazon gift card. That way, as he needs things throughout the year, he can order those things. For my mama, it's important that the gift is thoughtful. The only acceptable gift card is a thrift store gift card. It isn't a lazy, don't-think-about-it gift, it's what she wants. For her, a thrift store gift card is just perfect. She had to do a lot of thrifting as a mom with young kids, and she still loves doing it. As kids, our grandparents would give us a few dollars to help us buy things for Mama and Daddy, and they were both easy to please. To this day, anything with a butterfly on it is a winning gift in my mama's eyes. Simple pleasures still mean the most to the two of them.

Both my parents instilled in us the idea that even if you don't have much, you can still give. Among those meals we prepared at Christmas, many were reserved to help feed the homeless in our church community. My mama became a minister, and for her, one of the most important things you could give, something that didn't cost you a thing but time, was a prayer or a kind word. Daddy, who went to church but sometimes struggled with the notion of a church as part of a larger organization or institution, was more pragmatic. Handing out bottles of water and food to the people on the streets was his approach. Mama did that too, in her way, as part of more organized efforts through the church by hosting giveaways there. The lesson was clear: it doesn't matter the delivery system you use, just get out there and be of service to those in need.

My mama, in addition to being a minister, also led the music at our church. My brother is really talented and plays seven instruments. I don't know how—I don't think I'm much of a singer—but I was in the honor choir at school. (Mama "urged" me to join and may have exerted some influence!) Maybe the choir director heard about me at church when a bunch of us went to nursing homes and other places at Christmas to bring joy to the residents. Among those going there were my brother and sister, of course. They're both talented vocalists. Caroling was a big part of our Christmas season as well. I have to admit that I'm a big fan of R&B soul and Motown Christmas music along with all the hymns and carols. Christmas music is a big part of our celebration at church and at home.

I've had to work a few Christmas Days while at FOX, but I've been fortunate that the schedule has worked out well enough that I can get home to be with family. I'm still young, just twenty-eight, and I'm looking forward to the day when I can have kids of my own. I'd like to have a big family and establish Christmas traditions of our own. I know one thing: I'll do what my mama and daddy did for my siblings and me and be sure to teach my family about being charitable and having reasonable expectations. I'm not sure how I'll deal with the whole Santa issue, but I will work hard no matter who gets the credit and do all I can to make sure that no one will go hungry.

Lawrence Jones currently serves as a *FOX & Friends* Enterprise Reporter.

The
Joy of
Receiving

Ainsley Earhardt

*Christmas reminds Ainsley Earhardt of how the gifts
of love and generosity she received from her mother
and grandmother made the holiday so special.*

I grew up in South Carolina and had a wonderful childhood. We didn't have a lot, but we had enough and our family was happy. My mom was a schoolteacher and my dad was the head basketball coach at Wofford College in Spartanburg. It's funny that "Spartan" can mean simple, frugal, or sparse, because that word could easily fit my father, who is a saver, buys used cars, and doesn't spend unnecessarily. My parents did the best they could with their limited means to make sure that me; my older sister, Elise; and my baby brother, Trent, never went without. All my memories of Christmas and family are fond

The Earhardt family—Mom and Dad with Ainsley;
older sister, Elise; and younger brother, Trent.

ones as a result—and thanks to a lot of people. But there are several women who played crucial roles in helping me enjoy the Christmas spirit, which I am passing on to my own daughter.

My family made sure that we understood the importance of being generous no matter your circumstances. We moved to Columbia, the state capital, when I was in fourth grade. The neighborhood was friendly and we instantly formed bonds. We took care of one another and celebrated the holidays, including Christmas. Every home was decorated with white lights, and in each window the families placed a candle.

Some of my fondest memories of Christmas involve my mom; my sister, Elise; my aunt Lynn; and my grandmother being in the kitchen cooking or baking.

Christmas is my mother's favorite holiday. She is an excellent chef and baker. At Christmas, the four of us would bake and decorate Christmas cookies, which we shared with the neighbors. My sister and I were tasked with delivering them. Mom would stack pretty Christmas plates with our labors, and then Elise and I went door-to-door dropping them off to every family on our street.

You can't put a price tag on most of my cherished holiday memories.

My maternal grandmother, Mimi, was a tiny bit of a woman who stood no more than five feet one inch or five feet two inches tall. She had a great, loving heart and a real way about her. She reminded me of Nancy Reagan. She and my grandfather Pop were very social and gracious. I never heard them exchange a harsh word with each other or with anyone else for that matter.

At Christmastime, Mimi would make sure that she bought six presents for every grandchild. She also always wrapped them perfectly. She even taught all her grandchildren the ins and outs of wrapping a gift, to the point that we learned her secrets for folding the tissue paper just so and how to make the neatest, most precise bows. I couldn't really master her tissue-paper folding back then, but I marveled at those perfect folds and creases whenever I opened one of her gifts. Even as a child I appreciated the time she spent buying the gifts and also making sure each child received the same amount of presents. This way, we knew she loved us equally.

We spent Christmas Day with my extended family eating and enjoying one another's company. I can still picture Mimi and Pop sitting in chairs on the edge of the room when we gathered at their house. My grandparents always had a small faux tree. The grandchildren sat on the floor while our parents, aunts, uncles, and grandparents sat in chairs circling us to watch our excitement as we opened each gift. Along with the presents under the tree, envelopes hung from its branches. My grandparents would give each adult an envelope of cash. It couldn't have been much, although I never asked the amount. I just remember the tradition and feeling happy for them as they opened their individual envelopes.

Ainsley with "Mimi" and cousin, Henry.

When we lived in Spartanburg, we were only a thirty-minute drive from my grandparents' house. After we spent Christmas morning playing with the toys Santa generously delivered, we packed our bags and headed to Mimi and Pop's house in Greenville, South Carolina. We sat down for a memorable meal, visited, opened more gifts, and then headed to my mother's cousin's house. His name is Wesley. He always had a book of Life Savers candies ready for each child, which came with eight different flavors. The kids played games of pool in his garage, while the adults were drinking cocktails and visiting inside the house.

Mimi passed away when I was twenty-one years old. She was the first grand-parent I lost, and her death hit me hard. I was a junior in college and my memories of her have really stayed with me. Mimi would buy us all clothes. I know it sometimes doesn't go over well for kids when their grandparents try to find things that are fashionable, let alone wearable. That wasn't the case with Mimi. She bought me one outfit for Christmas when I was in middle school and I wore it the first day we returned to school after the holiday break. It included fuchsia-colored corduroy pants and a jewel-toned button-down flannel shirt. I would pop the collar and wear it untucked. Mimi bought me a necklace to go with it that featured the same colors. Little wooden pencils hung down from the chain. Each pencil was a different color to match the shirt perfectly. I thought the pairing was gorgeous and I was proud of my grandmother's cool taste in clothes. This was back in the eighties when we were wearing these crazy colors. And I will never forget that outfit. I kept it and cherished it for years.

I also remember, as a little girl, really wanting a doll I had seen in a store in Greenville, South Carolina. I would go into the store and just look at that baby doll perched on the top shelf. The clerk would take her down and allow me to hold her, as I so badly wished I were taking her home. For a year, I went into that store and looked up at the doll, imagining what it would be like to have her. My parents would buy us a few small things on some occasions like birthdays, but the price tag on this particular doll was more than my parents were willing to spend. The following Christmas, I was opening gifts at Mimi and Pop's house, carefully unwrapping one of my grandmother's exquisite packages. I caught a glimpse of the doll's beautiful hair. I'm pretty certain that my cry of delight and surprise was heard all over the house. I remember looking around as the adults blissfully watched us all from above and seeing Mimi's beaming smile of pleasure. I screamed out to my mother, "Look, Mama. Look what Mimi and Pop gave me. My doll!" I am certain my mom had a hand in directing Mimi toward this purchase, but I wasn't completely sure at my young age. I was thrilled and my heart was full. In truth, that's how Mimi made us all feel.

It's funny to think of this now, but Mimi's "treat them all equally" practices didn't get passed down to my mom and dad. I'm joking a bit about this but it's actually true and we all talk about it and none of us denies it or is offended by it. My little brother, Trent, is the favorite! It was obvious that my dad was thrilled to finally have a son, and my sister and I have a special bond, but Trent's my baby brother! My mother lights up whenever he's around. I still remember so well when my dad came to our school and told us that my mother had delivered a boy. Trent basically has three moms, my sister and I dote on him so much, then and now. My sister is three years older than me, and for five and a half years it was just the two us, so we had a good run there for a while.

Later on, when we came downstairs on Christmas morning, we'd find our presents laid out in the living room. This was after we'd made the move to Columbia. Dad had transitioned from coaching to sales (to make more money for his burgeoning family) and Mom was still teaching. It was clear to us that our fortunes had improved. We'd stand in the living room and look around. There, on one cushioned chair, Elise's presents sat stacked. Next to it, on a matching small chair, were mine. On the sofa, Trent's massive pile was sprawled out like a sleeping body. He'd get hunting gear, a BB gun or shotgun, games, basketballs, baseball equipment, electronics, and University of South Carolina–branded shirts, hats, and sweatshirts, which is where most everyone in my family graduated from college (and eventually my brother and I did too). One year, there was a long string that he had to follow from the sofa to the garage. The string eventually guided him to a go-kart! All the young boys in our community received them that year, and our street quickly became a racetrack for the children.

Just to put this in better context, before my parents' finances improved, and even after, my parents were pretty fiscally conservative. That's the polite way of saying it. My dad was legendarily frugal. He was a resident of "Spartan"-burg both literally and spiritually. I'd go back to school after Christmas and kids would talk about getting a VHS videotape player for the whole family. We got a

Beta machine and struggled at the local video store to find any movies to watch. Friends got an Atari video game console. We got a ColecoVision set. We enjoy talking and joking with Dad about his bargain hunting. Don't get me wrong, we loved the alternative gifts, appreciated everything they worked hard to provide, and knew Mom's and Dad's hearts were in the right place.

There was only one time when Dad's frugality caused any kind of fuss—briefly, that is. One year he came home with a very sad, bare-looking Charlie Brown–like Christmas tree. Mom took one look at it and said, "Wayne, what were you thinking? How can I decorate this tree? There are too many holes in it." Christmas meant so much to my mom, and decorating the house was such a big part of that. She was crushed when her Christmas tree was not perfectly shaped.

Dad looked sheepish and said, "Well, I felt sorry for it. It was in the very back of the farm all by itself."

By this time, even us kids had figured out Dad's usual method of operation. Laughing, we asked him, "Dad, how much of a discount did you get for it?"

In the end it didn't matter. Mom made do. We figured a way to turn it so that the most abundant part of the tree faced into the room and the barest parts faced the wall. Mom strategized the hanging of heavier ornaments on the branches above the holes, and ultimately we had a very presentable tree.

We took part in the neighborhood cookie exchange at Christmas. It was another way the community spread Christmas spirit every year. Each of the moms in our neighborhood, including my mother, Mrs. Saunders, Mrs. Camp, Mrs. Shackelford, Mrs. Henderson, and others would put out a plate of their specialty on a table. Then we'd take turns going around that huge spread of treats to fill up a plate to take home. As children, having our own plates of cookies was a huge treat that we so looked forward to. There was nothing better than a Christmas cornflake wreath cookie, a popular holiday treat in South Carolina.

The Camps always hosted a party on Christmas Eve. As a child, we would go to the annual event for about an hour, go to church, and hurry home to prepare milk and cookies for Santa. As we grew older, we would walk up the street to their house on Christmas Eve carrying to-go cups of wine to visit and celebrate with the neighborhood gang and stay until it was time to leave for church services. I appreciate just how much thought and effort went into the preparation and planning of each event. The way the Camps shared their love and joy of the season made the holiday special for everyone on our street and contributed to the many beautiful Christmas experiences.

One year we moved to Charlotte, North Carolina, because my dad received a job opportunity. We would live there for a year. He left coaching and went to work for one of his players' fathers. We were house hunting and found a pretty one-story white-brick home. The three children begged and begged my parents to buy it—for one reason. There was a hot tub on the back porch. To be honest, it could have been a tumbledown shack—it wasn't—but that hot tub had real curb appeal for my siblings and me.

I do recall that Christmas my mom had her eye on a coat that my dad bought for her. My parents weren't into public displays of affection, but every year when my mom opened her gift from my dad, they'd kiss. We didn't squirm or say, "Yuck." We just thought it was so sweet, and Mom and Dad were/are really great together and amazing parents to us. We loved Charlotte, but the Columbia, South Carolina, territory became vacant and his company allowed him to transfer "home"—to the city where he grew up. We said goodbye to the hot tub and looked forward to a new adventure back in our home state of South Carolina.

It was good to be back in the state where I was born and spent the first eight years of my life. I had so many fond memories of Spartanburg, and now we were returning to our roots in South Carolina.

In Spartanburg, the Lowrys were our next-door neighbors and, like us, they had three children—March, Brad, and David. They were our tree-climbing, fort-building, sledding-down-the-snowstorm-closed-street, bike-riding best friends. I shared a bedroom with either Elise or Trent at one point or another. We'd look out our windows across the way to the Lowry house. We'd wave to one another, and, on Christmas Eve, we'd signal to one another, making the "call me" gesture with our hands, urging them to contact us in the morning once they knew what Santa had delivered. I also remember (sorry, Elise, but it's true) after our signals to the Lowry children, I would have to climb into bed with my sister, no matter the room arrangements, to sleep with her. She was afraid of Santa Claus and needed my presence to make her feel safe. Maybe we should have posted Trent outside the door with his BB gun, but he was too young then and was still gunless.

And like kids everywhere, we woke up in the dark and went to our parents' room to beg them to let us see what Santa had brought us.

In Columbia we moved into a larger home. It was Dad's dream house, as he picked it out. This is where my parents still reside today—the street where we are very close with all the neighbors and celebrate Christmas as a group.

On Christmas morning, Elise, Trent, and I sat at the top of the stairs and waited for Dad to get the video camera ready to capture us making a mad dash for the gifts. Mom had to brush her teeth, make her coffee, and get situated in a chair in our den before we were allowed to come down.

I had a very all American and wonderful childhood. After we enjoyed our gifts from Santa, we opened gifts under the tree from our parents. Then we would get ready for the family to arrive. The day stretched on—a day that I never wanted to end and that continued to be full of festivities.

My aunt Lynn and uncle Robert would come over with my three male cousins and the cooking began. We always had turkey and beef tenderloin. Robert is a huge FOX News fan and is the master of the grill in our family. He grilled the meat and always carved the turkey. Each year, the delicious smell of the food grilling radiated throughout the neighborhood. And when it was finally time for dinner, our eyes lit up, belts were loosened, and smiles were spread around the dining room.

My aunt Lynn put out her made-from-scratch buttered biscuits. My mom displayed her sweet potato casserole (with roasted marshmallows on top, of course!), and Mimi's contribution, which we still make annually, was her amazing cornbread dressing and gravy.

The adults were sipping Coke, or it was being used as a mixer, or some other cocktail, because Pop was with the Coca-Cola Bottling Company for his entire career. The plant would sell lemonade to the employees only, and Mimi and Pop always provided it for the grandchildren.

Their house was loaded with Coca-Cola novelty items—a Coke-themed bread box, a radio in the shape of a soda machine, a silver bowl on top of the refrigerator that had Coke-bottle legs, a Tiffany Coke lamp. Pop was so proud of the Coca-Cola company and often took us with him to work. At Christmas, we all received Coke-themed ornaments, and they still hang from our Christmas trees. They were different each year and always featured Santa hoisting a bottle.

When Mimi and Pop died, it took a long time for my mom to get over their deaths. She missed them so much. I asked her why it was so hard for her, as we had always been taught and believed that they were in a better place. She said that was true, but she missed them so much because she was so grateful for everything they had done for her and the rest of our family. She mostly missed being able to pick up the phone and hear their voices. She described her own childhood as living in a bubble. They were protected from so many of the harsher realities of life. I understood that. I feel the same way about my childhood, about nearly every aspect of my life. We were all so fortunate, and it was so obvious to me that like nearly everyone, our parents wanted our lives to be better than theirs had been. They wanted to protect, to provide, to pass on traditions, to teach us to be kind, grateful, caring, and compassionate. All of those things were a part of our upbringing and they all seemed to really come together at Christmas.

Maybe that's why after Mimi died, it was at Christmas that I really, truly felt

her loss. I was sitting at my aunt and uncle's kitchen table in Rock Hill, South Carolina. This was the first year Mimi wasn't with us, and I just cried.

Pop passed away within a year of Mimi, and our family gathered in their home to clean out their belongings. It was so surreal to know they weren't upstairs or greeting us at the door. Mimi wasn't cooking in the kitchen and Pop wasn't coming in from a day of golf. The fireplace wasn't crackling and their voices were no longer heard. When we went through their books, the family wanted me to have Mimi's faith-based literature and her biblical studies. I flipped through the pages, and her copious notes were scribbled all over the margins. I was blown away by her knowledge of the Bible. I knew that she attended her Presbyterian church every Sunday. I often went with her and Pop to services. I knew that she was a very good person. But I had no idea she was such a strong Christian. Looking back, I should have. In fact, when Mimi was dying of cancer, her minister came into her hospital room. They held hands and recited scripture together. Until then I didn't know she had memorized scripture. She didn't talk about her faith, but she walked it daily. She was always a very private person. I was told by the family that she would have wanted me to have her books.

I felt like she was telling me something that she hadn't said to me when she was alive. That gift from her changed my life. I was beginning to get very involved in my church and learning the meaning of having a deep, personal relationship with Jesus Christ. I am still brought to tears thinking about her and the impact she had on our family. I am extremely grateful for the love she poured into my mother and the love she and my mom poured into me.

I am ashamed to say that there was a time growing up when I resented my mom. Now I realize just how blessed and fortunate I was and am. I feel awful that as a teenager I didn't realize how blessed I was or notice the amazing gifts my family continuously gave. My mom and I—our personalities—are different, but the greatest gift she gave me was allowing me the freedom to be who I am and loving me for who I became. I didn't get that then and sometimes felt as if she didn't support my dreams and big-city ambitions. I think she understood something about the nature of giving that I failed to comprehend. There are things we want and there are things we need. She gave me both, but sometimes the two came in conflict and needs won out over wants. She needed to protect me; I wanted to go my own way, to get to New York, for acting, performing, or being onstage in some capacity.

The last Christmas we all spent together, just before my mom suffered a debilitating stroke, we traveled to a beach house in South Carolina. My mom loves Christmas so much and loved hosting it, but she had some health issues, and I thought it would be a good idea to make things easier for her. She mentioned a place on the beach a number of times and thought I should look into renting the house for the holidays. I thought, "What a great gift for her." The place was spacious and beachfront and could accommodate the entire family, including our cousins and their children.

I remember having to leave just after New Year's Day because I had to be back at work in New York City. Hayden, my daughter (who looks just like my mom did at the same age), and I said our goodbyes and loaded up for the airport. As I was backing out of the driveway, Mom was standing in front of the door at the top of the stairs, crying and waving goodbye. She hated to see us go. She adores Hayden and all her grandchildren. The apple doesn't fall very far from the tree, and she has been so great with all the grandchildren like Mimi was. A month later she suffered a severe stroke.

The following Christmas, Mom was still very sick—unable to speak, walk, or do much on her own. We cherished that holiday and knew it would be very important to her to celebrate Christmas at her house surrounded by our family tree, traditions, family, and neighbors. My high school friends came. The Saunderses, Camps, Hendersons, Shackelfords, and many more stopped by. It was a special, family affair.

I'm grateful we were able to give her that Christmas and the others since. It is her favorite holiday—Jesus's birthday. And even though she lost most of her ability to speak, she still directs my dad as he decorates the tree and winds garland around the stair banisters. She lights up during those moments, and if I close my eyes, I can still picture her in the kitchen with Mimi and Aunt Lynn baking all those cookies, following family recipes and laughing through the stress of it all. I can see her reaching for the copy of *The Christmas Story* that sat on our coffee table. From years and years of use, that book's spine and cover are a bit tattered and torn, and I can hear her beautiful voice reading the story to us. I am transported back to Spartanburg, the Episcopal Church of the Advent, then our home in Columbia and Ebenezer Lutheran Church (where my dad also attended when he was growing up). I'm looking at the chrismons, these ornately beautiful ornaments that are hanging from the tall trees that flank the altar. That memory takes me back to the fourth or fifth grade, when our family spent much of our week working in or attending services. Dad and I were on the church council and Mom served on the vestry committee and was very involved in helping to decorate the church for Christmas. My memories of those chrismon ornaments are meaningful to me. I sat side by side with my mom, each of us sewing them after a church fire destroyed the originals. I know her fine-motor skills aren't the same anymore. But I am grateful we were able to contribute to the church in such a lovely way and know that our detailed, intricate ornaments are still being used in Ebenezer Church each Christmas.

I love to paint, and in first grade, I painted a huge picture of Santa Claus with the house in the background. I put cotton balls on the white parts of his hat. And one Christmas morning, I came downstairs and saw that Mom had it framed for me. She would put this huge picture of Santa over the mantel in our living room and year after year she took pleasure in hanging it. She still insists on displaying it each year. It is a sweet way to honor me. It meant a lot to me then but means more to me now.

Christmas plays a large part in our lives. It is the day Jesus was born and our family enjoys celebrating that very necessary and important holiday. He was born on Christmas and rose from the dead on Easter. His birth, death, and resurrection are the ultimate gift, and God the ultimate giver. We have only to receive with grateful hearts. Jesus paved the way for us and allowed everyone to have another chance, despite our transgressions. We are bound by love for God, for our family, and for the rest of His children. The way in which we celebrate may be different, but the spirit of Christmas endures forever. Thank you, Mimi, and thank you, Mom. You taught me well. I'm doing my best to live up to the example you set and hope I can pass your Christmas spirit on to your grandchildren and generations to come.

Ainsley Earhardt is the cohost of *FOX & Friends* (weekdays 6–9 a.m. ET).

Brian Kilmeade

It can be tough to get over it when you don't get the right man-eating monster, which is how Brian Kilmeade's feud with Santa began . . .

I had two brothers and I was the middle child. You can imagine what it was like in my house around Christmas with the three of us being pretty close in age. We fed off one another's anticipation for Santa's arrival. One year, when I was six, my mom was desperate to get us to sleep on Christmas Eve. She got us into bed, and to keep us there she said that if Santa spotted us downstairs before morning, he would take all our gifts away. We didn't want that to happen, of course, but we were too wound up to sleep. I shared a room with and spent much of the night talking to my brothers, Jimmy and Steven. We lay there in the dark chatting away, but exhaustion must have finally overtaken us. We fell asleep for a little while.

The Colossus Rex, the toy every kid wants.

When we woke up, the temptation was too great. We hopped out of bed and went to the top of the stairs. We spotted the gifts under the tree. So we were thinking to ourselves, "Santa was here. We're going to go down to see what's going on." We were down there, and all of a sudden we heard banging noises. We figured it had to be Santa. Remembering what my mother had told us, we darted back upstairs, afraid we might lose our gifts. I got back in bed and lay there listening for more Santa sounds. I didn't hear any. I checked with my brothers and they said they didn't hear anything either. We went back downstairs. I felt a bit of a breeze. Wrapping paper rustled. I looked and saw that the front door to the house was open. I closed the door and locked it. We went back upstairs and went to bed.

I don't know if it was fear or having been up most of the night, but we slept solidly the rest of the morning. In fact, my mom had to wake us up at seven.

"But"—to slightly modify the tagline of the legendary broadcaster Paul Harvey—"that's not the rest of the story."

We only found out the truth a couple of years later, when the threat that Santa Claus may take away gifts from too-eager children no longer struck fear in our hearts. We didn't believe in Santa anymore. Even though what had become known as "the door-was-open Christmas" had proceeded smoothly, my parents thought it was time to let us know another Christmas truth. It was time to reveal that the noise we heard that night wasn't Santa Claus and his eight reindeer. It was my father and his six-cylinder Chevy Nova. He'd come home from work, and my parents had hidden the gifts either in his car or in the garage. In any case, he was ferrying presents into the house. He'd dropped off a few and gone back outside for more. That's when I entered the picture and shut the door and locked it. My dad couldn't get in the house. This was before cell phones, so he couldn't call my mom privately. Instead, not wanting to wake us all up by banging on the door and potentially spoiling the whole Santa Claus story, he eventually drove to a pay phone and called home. None of us, including my mom, heard the phone ring.

Still wanting to keep up the pretense of the Santa story, and figuring that if a phone ringing wasn't enough to rouse anyone from their sleep, his only option was to wait out the night. He settled into the Nova's interior. There was no heat in the car, so he spent a couple of hours in the freezing cold, shivering. Finally, now desperate to get warm, he resorted to the tried-and-true seen-it-in-the-movies approach. He crept around the house and tossed little rocks against the window of his and my mom's bedroom. For some reason that plinking sound was enough when a phone's ringing wasn't. My mom woke up and let him in.

More important, at least to me as a kid, was that he brought in the rest of the gifts, and we were, until he shared this with us, none the wiser. That's a parent's dedication.

But then, as he finally revealed the truth to us, he said there was still something puzzling him. He had no idea how the door ended up closed. I couldn't lie. I said it was me. Thinking back on it, I was absolutely certain that the door being open had nothing to do with Santa. After all, he was a well-known second-story break-in guy. We had a fireplace. We had a chimney. Santa doesn't do doors; therefore, door open means door closed. How many times in my life had I heard, "Make sure you close the door behind you"? Turns out "Santa" was the guy who made the mistake of not following our house rules.

That wasn't the only time Santa messed things up. One year, after a thorough examination of all the Christmas catalogs and TV commercials peddling the latest and the greatest toys, I decided that I had to have a vinyl action figure from a series called Outer Space Men. The one I really wanted was Colossus Rex. I didn't care about the rest of the men in the series; I didn't care about what part of space those other guys were from. Colossus Rex was the guy for me. Just say the word "C-O-L-O-S-S-U-S" and you'll understand why. He was the biggest and baddest of the bunch, and images of a T. rex–like guy terrorizing the universe came to mind. He was from Jupiter. He had a lizard-like head with gills. Most of all he was cut. His chest and arms were enormously muscled; he was the spaceman equivalent of the Incredible Hulk, with a physique and fury to match,

It wasn't an enormously expensive, extravagant gift, but I really wanted that Colossus Rex. I could rule the universe with my mighty muscles. Come Christmas morning, once my dad had slept a couple of hours after getting home late from working at the bar, we all gathered around the tree. I chose one of my presents based on its size and shape, figuring it was very close to the packaging I'd seen for Colossus Rex in the Sears catalog. I tore off the paper and there he was in all his splendor—Metaluna Mutant.

That's right. Say those words. "M-E-T-A-L-U-N-A M-U-T-A-N-T." His mutation was obvious. He was a tall, wiry guy with lobster-claw hands. His enormous brain encompassed the outside of the skull. Red veins ran through the folds of gray matter. He was hideous, and not in a good way. Nothing mattered to me more than my disappointment. How could Santa have not gotten it into his brain that I wanted Colossus Rex, the man of muscle, and not this freakish brainiac? If this were *Star Trek*, Colossus Rex was Captain Kirk. Metaluna Mutant was Mr. Spock. Who wanted to be Mr. Spock?

My disappointment was obvious. I was devastated. My dad stepped in. He told me that Santa hadn't made a mistake. He thought that the big guy from the North Pole was trying to teach me a life lesson. Metaluna Mutant had a big brain. He had to be super smart. Sure, Colossus Rex was super strong, but in life you were better off being smart than strong. As the years passed, I didn't develop into a physical behemoth. I did have some smarts, though, so I guess my dad was right. I've done okay in life.

I once told this story on air, and a viewer rushed in to fill the void that was colossal childhood disappointment. He was a toy collector and he sent me a Colossus Rex.

Brains.

Muscle.

It's good to have them both. Now the beauty part of that equation . . .

It actually got worse. The very next year, my parents bought a Colossus Rex. Was I delighted? Were my dreams fulfilled?

No.

My brother Jimmy was the recipient of the muscled marvel.

So, um, Dad, what was that you were saying about how it was better to have brains than brawn? What bells from that teachable moment weren't ringing true now?

My dad worked hard. Christmas Eve was a big deal at the bar he worked at since it allowed eighteen-year-olds in to legally drink. College kids came home for the holiday and they stayed late into the night and early on Christmas morning. Dad was a trooper, though. He'd come home, get a little bit of sleep, or sometimes not, go through the gift opening, and then grab a few hours of rest before our house was crammed with people and food.

My mother is Italian and she and my two aunts were in charge of meal preparation. They'd convene a meeting in the days leading up to Christmas and formulate a game plan. They then executed it to perfection. Feeding as many as fifty people, making all of it by hand, from appetizers to desserts, took so much effort. They did it with love, and I still feel a bit guilty whenever we order out for a birthday party or other get-together.

My aunt Ellen's Swedish meatballs were outstanding. They battled for attention and praise with my mother's Italian version. I can't declare a winner. I can declare a couple of losers, however. There's a reason why Campbell's doesn't sell dandelion soup. Also, you shouldn't serve something that is best used as bait to catch something else aquatic. We had eel for no reason that I could figure. I guess it's a delicacy, but it's all a question of taste. In this case, something that tasted bad. What never tasted bad were the struffoli, Italian honey ball cookies, that my mom and her sisters made. Rolled with sprinkles, they can't ever disappoint anyone's taste buds.

Swedish Meatballs

Meatballs

3 tablespoons butter or margarine,
divided, plus more as needed
3 tablespoons finely chopped onion
¾ cup light cream
¾ cup packaged dry bread crumbs
½ pound ground pork

1½ pounds ground chuck
2 large eggs, slightly beaten
2 teaspoons salt
¼ teaspoon pepper
¼ teaspoon ground allspice
Dash of ground cloves

Sauce

2 tablespoons flour
½ cup light cream
1 teaspoon salt

Dash of pepper
½ teaspoon bottled gravy seasoning

1. **Meatballs:** Melt 1 tablespoon of butter in a skillet over medium heat, then add the onions and sauté 3 minutes or until golden. Remove from the heat and set aside. In a large bowl, combine the cream, ¾ cup water, and the bread crumbs. Add the onion, ground meats, eggs, salt, pepper, allspice, and cloves—toss lightly to mix well.

2. With a teaspoon, shape the mixture into 75 meatballs, about ¾ inch in diameter. Melt 2 tablespoons of butter in the same skillet over medium heat and sauté the meatballs, a few at a time, until browned on all sides. Add more butter as needed. Remove the meatballs to a plate lined with a paper towel and set aside.

3. **Sauce:** Remove all but 2 tablespoons of drippings from the skillet and set over low heat. Stir in the flour until smooth. Gradually stir in the cream and 1½ cups of water and bring to a boil, stirring constantly, then reduce the heat to low. Add the salt, pepper, and gravy seasoning. Add the meatballs and heat gently for 5 minutes or until heated through.

I also think it's important to have other kinds of family traditions. I understood this early on. When I was twelve, my oldest cousin got married and his wife joined us for gift giving. I presented her with a T-shirt that said "I'm Related to Brian Kilmeade." This was the coveted item, the Colossus Rex of T-shirts. Every year I would give someone a T-shirt or personalized item that was somehow in praise of me. Everyone enjoyed my less-than-serious, out-of-control-ego gifting. Over time, I'd add to the "I'm related to" line with things like "I'm the second-oldest in the family, but the best news is I'm related to Brian Kilmeade." The slogans got so long that the printer ran out of room on the front and had to use the back to complete the job.

At least none of my relatives ever suffered the fate of Frosty the Snowman. As a kid I watched the usual Christmas shows, but Frosty really received a frosty reception. I mean, who in their right mind would think that kids would enjoy seeing a show about a snowman come to life who then gets caught in a hothouse and is reduced to a carrot, glasses, a pipe, and a couple of articles of clothing? I'd watch it, of course, and sit there thinking, "There's no way he's coming back from this."

For me it was the wholesome Walton family *Homecoming* that warmed my heart and sent the right Christmas message. I liked how they lived on their own mountain, and their rustic lifestyle had some appeal. They were living in the Depression era, and in a way I could relate to that. We always got real Christmas trees at a gardening center. The tree still had its roots attached. We were a little ahead of the environmental curve on this one, because after Christmas was over, we'd plant the tree in the backyard. They weren't the biggest or the best trees, but at least they could be planted. I liked seeing them all lined up in the backyard, and they brought back great memories year-round. Even the year we were a little short on funds and had to dig up a previous year's tree and bring it back in the house to decorate.

With the Italian side of the family, my mom's—the D'Andrea clan—came a lot of traditions and excitement. The Irish side was a little more reserved. One of the tree-related traditions we carried out was using ornaments that had been given as gifts or passed down from a previous generation. Decorating the tree was fun, but assembling the tracks for the Lionel train that ran around it was even better. I don't know if it's an immutable law of the universe or not, but toy train derailments always seemed to happen on the far side of the tracks. I can still feel the needles scratching me as I crawled under the tree to get the thing back on track. I've kept up the tradition of having a tree and a train with my kids, and that means a lot to me. Instead of having a big multi-family event on Christmas Day, we do that on Christmas Eve. Just my wife, Dawn, and me and the kids. I've been fortunate to not have to work Christmas Eve or Day like my dad so often did. That way I never run the risk of being locked out of the house.

Obviously, I like to laugh and make people laugh and that's sometimes the trait that we always think of first with Santa—the man is jolly, right? He likes to spread joy as much as he does gifts.

Turns out his brother was a pretty good guy also. That's why one of my favorite holiday movies is *Fred Claus*. It's got a great cast, Santa's unsung brother gets the attention he deserves, and we learn that Santa isn't perfect. Santa could learn something from Fred—like the fact that there's a colossal difference between Colossus Rex and Metaluna Mutant. Not even close, Santa. You should know better. Next time, ask your brother; maybe he's the one with the brains in the family.

Brian Kilmeade is the cohost of *FOX & Friends* (weekdays 6–9 a.m. ET).

John Roberts

*John Roberts appreciates happy Christmases all the more
because he remembers a Christmas that wasn't.*

I'm enormously grateful that, for the vast majority of Christmases I experienced, I have only positive moments to now reflect on. I know that's not true for lots of other people. Whether because of loss or hardships, some people haven't enjoyed Christmas as much as I have. The holiday season for me hasn't been perfect, mind you, but compared to what others go through, I've been very, very fortunate. Still, I can empathize with those less fortunate people because the one Christmas I had that was far from perfect, far from good, was a very painful one for my family and me. It was also the one that taught me some very valuable

John Roberts and his twins, Kellan and Sage, at the White House.

lessons about perseverance and rising above tough circumstances. Those are important lessons, and I've never forgotten them.

My father died in late November 1962, right before I turned six years old. He had a congenital defect in his aorta, the main and largest artery that distributes blood throughout the body. Because of his condition, he had high blood pressure in his chest and head and low blood pressure in his legs and feet. He worked a high-stress job, and he was, as I recall, a pretty high-strung guy. How much his health concerns contributed to that is difficult to say, but one day at work he had an aneurysm. He was rushed to the hospital for emergency surgery, which he survived. Then my mom came home from the hospital, stood in the middle of the living room with my brother, my sister, and me, and said simply, "Daddy died."

As a five-year-old, it was difficult to process that sort of a blow. My sister, my mother, and I all huddled together. I could feel them quaking from their tears. My older brother was at the dining room table, where he'd been doing his homework. I heard his pencil drop. It was like that sound voiced the concern that we all had: "Okay, where do we go from here?"

I don't know if my mother knew immediately the answer to that question, but in time, God bless her, she sure made things happen. She worked long hours at simple jobs for little pay, but she made our lives work. She is the reason why I enjoyed a pretty good life growing up. She set me on the track to later success. We did not have many material things, but I believe that's a good thing for a child to experience and to learn from. If you have everything handed to you as a child, you'll never learn how to make things happen for yourself.

As a kid I appreciated what she did for us, but I don't think that until I was older and on my own did I fully understand how difficult a task she'd taken on. My mom was a housewife, a traditional housewife of the 1950s and 1960s. That meant she didn't work outside the home. She stayed there to take care of us. When she was younger she had been a hairdresser, but she hadn't done that kind of work for years. Suddenly she was thrown out into the working world because her husband had died and she had three children to provide for. Unsure of what to do, her first thought was that she would probably have to move us out of the house we had grown up in and into a small apartment somewhere else in Toronto, but somebody—it might have been one of my relatives—talked her out of that idea and advised her to do everything she could to hold on to our house. To her credit she worked some very hard jobs so that we could still live in that home.

She was a cashier at a pharmacy and a receptionist at a car dealership. She made ninety dollars a week.

Somehow she also managed to make that first Christmas work for all of us. While we didn't receive much in the way of gifts because there wasn't much money to go around, the greatest gift she gave us was to keep that roof over our heads. And she did it not just for that year but for every year until we all grew up and left the house. In fact, she hung on to that house until she was ninety-three years old and had to go into a home because of Alzheimer's. But God bless her for all she did for my siblings and me.

I learned very valuable lessons from her that Christmas, and those lessons were to believe in yourself, to work hard, to know the value of a dollar, and to live up to your commitments. So that was probably—from the standpoint of life lessons and their effect on your life—the seminal Christmas for me. Thankfully, I learned those difficult and painful lessons early on.

You never completely put a loss like that behind you. I thought I did, but each year as Christmas approached, even into my forties, this strange sadness would settle over me even though there were so many reminders of Christmas cheer. I thought about the reasons for that, and many were tied to my father's death. My mom, understandably, thought I was too young to go to my father's funeral. So I was left with this: my father went to work one day and never came back. I didn't get to see him ever again. I didn't get to say goodbye. My sorrow hung with me for a long, long time. I'd keep a lot of it to myself; I didn't want to spoil anyone's holiday. Besides, I did have so much else to be thankful for. A similar thing happened later on in life when I split with my first wife in the months before the Christmas season. It was sad, but we did what my mother had done. We did our best to make sure the kids had a happy Christmas. It was difficult, but I thought of what my mom had gone through and how well she had handled it.

You can get through things, but that doesn't mean you get over them. That also doesn't mean that the sadness and the joy of the season can't coexist.

Despite our hardships, when I was growing up Christmas was very important, and I looked forward to the day that my mom would say, "It's time to put up the Christmas lights." I remember in our little bungalow just outside of Toronto we had a picture window in the living room that faced the front of the house, and we had a string of lights that would go around that window. I so looked forward every year to being out there with my mom, putting up this string of lights. It was the same faded string of colored lights with orange and blue and green and red, and it would frame the window with a burst of color. Then we'd take an old, threadbare wreath with a single electric candle light and hang it from a little nail on the inside of the window so it sat perfectly in the middle of the window. I was always so happy as a child to put up those lights, because that really signified that Christmas was on the way.

We put up a fresh tree every year until my mother got a little bit older, and years after I moved out of the house she bought an artificial tree because it was much easier for her. But my mother was the most extraordinary of resourceful people. She would actually go get a Christmas tree at a hardware store some miles away and then bring it back on the bus. She also did that with an eight-foot ladder when she was ninety years old, but that's another story.

My mom always sacrificed to make sure there was something special for us when we woke up on Christmas morning. I'd wake up and there would be a stocking at the end of my bed. And when I say "a stocking," it was an actual stocking. Mother would take one of her stockings and fill it with little goodies. I didn't have a red knit stocking with a fuzzy trim around the top that had my name on it. I had a woman's stocking. And that nylon stocking was great because it was big, so there was a lot in it. I remember there would be a pair of gloves in it, there'd be a pair of socks, there'd be a book, and there'd be some little trinkets and maybe a baseball, things like that.

I always used to love digging to the very end, the very toe of the stocking, because—at Christmastime—my mother would go to the grocery store to buy a whole box of mandarin oranges, and at the toe of the stocking, she would put a mandarin orange. That was like my Christmas-morning prize, getting to the bottom of the stocking to find the orange. I would sit there on my bed with the baseball and the pens and pencils and things that were in my stocking strewn about on my bed. I'd eat that mandarin orange like it was the most special thing in the world.

I'm very fortunate to have remarried, and I once again have younger children. I loved the time when my adult children were still in the believe-in-Santa mode, and I'm fortunate that I get to go through those magical years again. My wife, Kyra, and I want to make sure our kids have the same kinds of great associations with Christmas that the two of us have. So, for me, reproducing that stocking moment was very important. (I admit that we don't use actual women's hosiery, but the point is still the same.) The kids' stockings hang by the fireplace, but then on Christmas Eve, Kyra and I do all kinds of elfish things. Put it this way, we probably should use nylon stockings, because the traditional ones don't expand enough to hold all the goodies we try to cram in there. So we do take the stockings up to their rooms and put them on the beds, and for the things that don't fit in the actual stockings, we arrange them nicely.

One tradition my mom had that Kyra and I haven't kept up, but one I have very fond memories of, was her Christmas pudding. She would bake it in a dome-shaped baking dish, and she'd serve it with a special cream sauce. Besides a cup of suet (which would now likely give me an instant heart attack), the secret ingredient—well, it wasn't really a secret since she told us it was in there—was coins. Before she baked the Christmas pudding, she'd sanitize and place the money in the cake batter. There wouldn't be a coin in every slice, so you can imagine the kind of competitiveness and envy that tradition produced. But as kids we loved the dessert, and getting the money, pardon the expression, was the icing on the cake.

One time I don't think my mother was counting her pennies was when I was twelve years old. This was a combination Christmas-birthday gift, but it remains my second-favorite gift of all time. It was something called a SnoKart, a sled that

was supposed to be a safer way to negotiate the steep hill at a nearby golf course. We'd slide down a section of its winding cart path where our toboggan would careen off course into the trees. We avoided serious injury, but our inability to negotiate those turns was frustrating.

Ice played a role in this escapade, and one year the SnoKart gave me the thrill of a lifetime. It handled turns really well, and I was hurtling along like I was piloting an Olympic bobsled. We've all seen that event on TV, and the Olympians have a brakeman to bring them to a stop. Well, I gave it an Olympian effort and pulled up on the brake lever of the SnoKart to no discernible effect. I got close to the edge of the track, which had been worn in by whoever had traveled the farthest down the hill. I sailed past that point, flew off the edge and into the air. I hung in the air like Superman for a long and glorious moment before landing some ten to fifteen feet beyond the end of the track, like a human arrow thrust into a snowbank. Perhaps a less graceful landing than Superman's, but I was ecstatic! I'd achieved the power of flight on a budget.

Obviously then, my first-favorite gift had to be pretty special to top that one, and it was. I love music and was, for a time, a veejay on Canada's version of MTV called MuchMusic. But at thirteen, I couldn't have imagined there'd be such a thing as music videos. I loved playing the guitar and Mother knew this very well. She saved up enough money to buy a used 1964 Fender Telecaster from a coworker. If you're not a guitar aficionado, a Telecaster is pretty close to the Holy Grail of stringed instruments. I cherished that guitar. I wish I still had it, especially in light of a recent Christmas gift Kyra purchased for me. She was able to secure guitar lessons for me from Joel Hoekstra, who is the lead guitarist from Whitesnake and frequently tours with the Trans-Siberian Orchestra. The latter's take on Christmas music is very distinctive.

As a music lover, I can't help but enjoy most Christmas songs. I like traditional carols, of course, but one of the more meaningful songs for me is "Do They Know It's Christmas?"—one that various musicians, under the leadership of Bob

Geldof, put out as part of the 1984 Band Aid effort to contribute to famine relief in Africa. That song really turned on for me the spirit of giving, as it did for many, many people, and put in better perspective the good fortune that we in the developed world enjoy. It is now decades old, but every time I hear it around Christmastime, I'm immediately brought back to the moment I first heard it and the resonance it had with me and so many others. My musical tastes are somewhat eclectic, and as much as I enjoy the serious theme of the Band Aid song, Kenny Chesney's "All I Want for Christmas Is a Real Good Tan" is a lot of fun. My son has learned to play drums and my daughter the piano. Though it wasn't for Christmas, at a fundraiser for their school I got to play along with them performing Journey's "Don't Stop Believin' " as the finale. What a treat to play music with the kids! We do that at the house too, and if we're not playing it live, we have it on the sound system all during the Christmas season and beyond.

The movie *Love Actually* is a favorite in our household. We watch it a number of times around the Christmas holiday. It really does demonstrate the spirit of Christmas, and even though there are a few risqué moments that aren't fully "young-children appropriate," the whole family watches it—at least most of it. I guess we keep some old-fashioned traditions like the stockings, and others are more contemporary like that film. We've also ventured into new Christmas food territory. This past year, we served friends sushi that we sliced and prepared ourselves.

We haven't abandoned the "old ways" entirely, just made a few menu adjustments. One way that we preserve our memories is by purchasing ornaments that are mementos of places we have traveled. So when we put our Christmas tree together, it's basically a cornucopia of our histories, whether it be Kyra's or mine or ours together. She brought with her to our home all the Christmas ornaments she made when she was in grade school. They're rudimentary in a way, and a lot of people would say, "Why are you hanging that on the tree?" But they're memories from her childhood. The kids have contributed their own handcrafted ones, and we enjoy adding them to the collection and putting them on display.

So we've got memories from childhood; we've got memories from trips; we've got meaningful ornaments shaped like guitars. As a result, every little piece of our tree tells a story of a portion of our lives. I think that that is a tremendous tradition for people to begin at a very early age. Because when you get to be my advanced age, the whole history of your life is there for everybody to see on your tree, and it's meaningful. Everything that's decorated for the Christmas season is a piece of your life that's on display.

We've also put ourselves on display, so to speak, in recent years. Kyra and I play non-dancing roles in the Washington Ballet's production of *The Nutcracker*. Kyra plays the Merry Widow. I play the Ambassador. The Washington Ballet's version is very DC-centric. It takes place in Georgetown, and well-known historical figures are characters in it. I've always loved *The Nutcracker*, so it's just a blast to be an actual part of it onstage. We've taken the kids to see it, and among the things on my wish list is to be in the audience when it is performed in New York at the New York City Ballet.

Also, at home we go for hay rides at a farm and enjoy hot chocolate there while we wait in line for the kids to see Santa Claus. Still, there's nothing like Christmas in New York City. That's almost a universal rule. But during one of our more memorable Christmases, in 2009, Manhattan and the rest of the city's boroughs were the last place you wanted to be. Kyra and I had plans to visit her mother in San Diego. This would be the first Christmas that the two of us would spend together. A huge snowstorm slammed the area, a truly hellacious winter storm. Still, I thought, this is New York. Of course they'll be able to clear the runways and roadways. I had to work in the days leading up to Christmas, so I didn't have a lot of flexibility about booking a flight that would get me to San Diego in time. As it turned out, so many flights were canceled that I thought I was not going to be able to get out west. While I was doing that, Kyra was working her magic. She found one flight leaving from Newark, and I was able to get on it. Kyra's resourcefulness was rewarded, and she saved Christmas for us.

This close call underlines again for me how lucky I've been to benefit from miracle workers at Christmas. Maybe they weren't as supernatural as Clarence Odbody from *It's a Wonderful Life*, but they've put in twice the work to make Christmas happen for the rest of us. It may be more blessed to give than receive, but it's still pretty blessed to receive.

We all got a bit of a reminder this past year about the true meaning of Christmas and how fortunate we are. At our church, there was a giving tree on display. Hanging from it were tags with gifts that local children had wished for. Some of the gifts were the obvious kinds of things—toys, video games, and such. The wishes that really got to my family were when kids were asking for the basics—socks, underwear, toiletries—the typical things we think of as being "bad" gifts to get at Christmas. Imagine the kind of life the kids who asked for those necessities must be living. Instead of going out to shop for the fun items, we selected the tags that revealed kids were in serious need. We knew the kids' ages and genders, so we got them things they could actually use—lots and lots of them. Next year we plan to add to their wish list with some toys; no kid should be without fun things at Christmas. I never was, my kids never were, and we want to do whatever we can to make sure the same is true for as many kids and their families as we can. That's the merriest kind of Christmas I can think of.

John Roberts currently serves as the coanchor of *America Reports* (weekdays, 1–3 p.m. ET).

Sandra Smith

Amid the chaos, Sandra Smith remembers to be
grateful for the quiet moments at Christmas.

It's Black Friday . . . the leftovers have cooled, the dishes are done, and the guests have gone home. At last, the Christmas decorating can begin. The time has unofficially come to gently dig out the family heirloom ornaments, homemade decorations, and bright lights and ribbons. It is everything I need to get into the holiday spirit. As an adult now with young children, this is a moment of pure joy for me. My favorite time of year is upon us, the Christmas season. So cue the music, light the fire, and pour me a cup of hot cocoa. And only now can I truly begin to enjoy it.

As a young journalist, I spent more than a few Black Fridays reporting on the biggest shopping day of the year. For most, that meant the official start to the

Sandra Smith with husband, John, and children, Cora and Johnny.

shopping season. But for me, that meant reporting *live* from retail stores and strip malls across the country starting as early as 5 a.m. Standing all day in front of cameras, commenting on crowd sizes and doorbuster bargains, and interviewing shoppers, I reported on the health of the economy, judging by turnout. A stark contrast to the days of my childhood eating leftovers and watching football. This, however, was my job and equal in importance to any other assignment.

I'll never forget the line of shoppers that wrapped half a mile long around an outlet mall in New York for a new Coach bag. Or that time I was assigned to re-port from a Sears department store in Chicago that decided to open its doors at 3 a.m. No one showed up for that ambitious opening time but us! Many of these assignments meant hopping on a plane from my hometown outside Chicago and heading back to work in New York late on Thanksgiving night while the turkey was still hot and the pumpkin pie had yet to be served. I remember being envious of those who settled in for a long winter's nap following the big feast, whereas I was touching down into Christmas season the following day. I knew my turn would come someday, and when it did, I'd be ready.

My yearning for a calm Christmas began while I was growing up in a big family—I am the youngest of six kids, my dad the eldest of ten, so the holidays were always pretty hectic. Mom running around the stores, Dad's last-minute shopping, the wrapping of last-minute gifts, and siblings fussing over setting up the tree. As a kid, I remember desperately wanting a real tree. But our family's tradition was putting together an artificial tree—my mom wouldn't budge on it. All the while, I stopped to wonder, did anyone notice I was still little and still believed in the magic of Christmas? Well, sadly, that came to a screeching halt at a very early age.

At age seven, as I was usually instructed to do for holiday meals hosted at our home, I headed to the laundry room to iron napkins for the dining room table. A tedious chore, but I didn't mind. However, while reaching for the iron, I discov-ered a not-well-hidden bag of presents neatly stored beneath the basement stairs. I was elated seeing the toys and dolls I had requested, but realized in that same moment that these were items only Santa could have known I asked for. I wrote, sealed, and sent letters to him—not my parents. Sigh. That discovery changed Christmas for me. The magic of Santa disappeared, but thankfully the spirit of the Christmas season did not.

Each year I looked forward to our tradition of about fifty-plus extended family members gathering for Christmas Eve. We would celebrate at the nearby houses of one of my aunts, uncles, or cousins, or at my childhood home, where my parents still live today. The location would change, but the traditions remained the same. Every year someone (usually my dad) would dress up as Santa Claus and make a grand entrance to the delight of little ones. Bells ringing, kids singing, piano playing, the magic of Christmas was alive and well for the Smiths. The family's investment in a head-to-toe Santa suit, bells, and an enormous gift sack paid off, and all were excited for his arrival, even the adults, who over the years would be called up to Santa's lap to reveal their Christmas wishes. There we were, each year, in our sweaters, munching on holiday treats and sipping hot apple cider. Sounds perfect, right?

Christmas morning came. We ate breakfast before dressing in our holiday best and heading out to a big Christmas mass at our local Catholic church. Stuffed from Mom's scrambled eggs and coffee cake, all eight of us crammed into a church pew, sang from the hymnal, and giggled as we missed words to prayers. . . . Those times were really special to me as a child. Wonderful memories. Warm fuzzies resulted. But my immediate family of eight assembled less and less over the years. My four sisters and brother were busy growing families of their own. Those Christmas mornings when all of us were together became rare. And as I grew older I began to feel like something was missing. I couldn't put my finger on it, but I would find out later.

Fast-forward years later to the eve of Christmas Eve 2009. I was working as a reporter for FOX. This was the night I was supposed to become engaged to my now-husband, John. I was still living in New York, while John remained in Chicago. We regularly flew back and forth to see each other on weekends, but we made it our tradition to always be together for the holidays in Chicago, where our families were concentrated. In my usual frenzy with work and a busy schedule, I missed my flight home that year, ruining John's wedding proposal plan and special dinner to follow—to the disappointment of not only his family but mine as well. My mother was in on it, and John's mother, who had passed down a family diamond for the big moment. Everyone knew, except me.

Still in New York, I jumped on a plane the following day, landing in Chicago on Christmas Eve, feeling very behind and crunched for time. I arrived with a list of to-dos that took most of the day ahead of family celebrations, delaying John's proposal backup plan. He struggled to find the right moment to pop the question. He eventually did, suggesting that we exchange gifts just before we departed for the Smith family Christmas Eve. It may not have been the perfectly planned moment he anticipated, but it was the best Christmas present I ever received. That moment continues to keep the Christmas season near and dear to my heart. We looked forward to sharing the news with family that evening. Aunts and uncles cheered as we gathered for the Smith dinner party, and when we made it to John's mother's traditional Christmas Eve later that night, the happy celebration continued.

While these were all special moments in our lives, they all felt so hurried and rushed. No time to stop and smell the poinsettias, if you will. But then at least, we had a plan. With a ring on my finger, a wedding date on the books, and the hope of one day settling into our own family traditions, things were looking up. I had visions of sugar plums dancing in my head, but never dreamed just how picturesque our future settings would be . . .

Imagine a snow-blanketed valley that inspired Irving Berlin to write the song "White Christmas" back in 1940. Well, that's where my precious family of four (five including our dog) has settled in to create our own Christmas memories and traditions. The calm I'd been seeking, and whatever I had felt was missing over the years, has arrived. As I hoped for, the Christmas spirit stays alive and the magic is back.

Nestled in the Catskill Mountains, we head out every year on a hunt for the perfect Christmas tree. A real tree chosen by us, cut down with our own saw, dragged to the car, tied down with rope, and driven home . . . in stark contrast to those lovely but hectic Christmases of my childhood. Trees so fresh the smell instantly fills the air. It is the imperfections of those country trees that I have come to love, reminding me of the benefits of a slower way of life. One I can only now start to appreciate.

And now a moment my kids and I both love: decorating our tree and gently rediscovering those family heirloom ornaments. Each telling a story, showing the twelve days of Christmas, and bringing such joy to all of us. The sparkle of each ornament lights the room. As we hang the old, we also fetch out the new ornaments, handmade by my two young children over the years. With every year that passes, each ornament is a sweet memory of Christmases gone by. We are interrupted only by the sizzle from the kitchen of the krumkake iron, a tool for making Scandinavian cookies from a recipe handed down by my children's grandmother. We delight in counting thirty seconds for each cookie to cook just right before peeling it off the iron and shaping it with a traditional krumkake roller. After cooling and sprinkling each with a bit of powdered sugar, perfection is reached and memories are made forever.

Krumkake

Requires a traditional two-sided Scandinavian cookie iron.

4 large eggs
1 cup sugar
½ cup (1 stick) butter, melted and cooled
½ teaspoon vanilla extract
½ teaspoon ground cardamom
1½ cups flour

1. In a medium bowl, beat the eggs and sugar, but do not overbeat. Stir in the cooled melted butter, vanilla, and cardamom. Add the flour and mix. The batter will have a cookie dough–like consistency.

2. Place 1 heaping teaspoon of batter on the grid, or make 1-inch round balls to place on the grid. Makes about 60 krumkake. Bake for approximately 30–40 seconds, depending on your preference for browning or the consistency of your batter.

3. Remove the krumkake from the grid with a spatula. If flat krumkake are desired, place the cookie on the countertop to cool. If you wish to shape your krumkake, do so immediately after removing from the grid using a wooden roller, such as the end of a wooden spoon. For a cone shape, use a wooden cone roller. Repeat with the remaining batter.

It's time to head to the little white church in the valley, where the kids use the full weight of their bodies to ring the bell as members of the community enter to sing traditional Christmas carols with friends and neighbors. A beautiful moment for all as we hold candles and sing under the kerosene chandelier usually lit by my husband. The addition of a piano player in that tiny little church dating back to the 1800s adds a special touch to a church already filled with spirit.

As night falls, we head home to prepare for Santa. First, we read our favorite Christmas books. Topping the list is Tasha Tudor's *The Night Before Christmas*, a clear family favorite. With our spirits high and the anticipation building, we set out homemade cookies for Mr. Claus and carrots for his reindeer. Our children make sure to remind their father not to light a fire since Santa is coming. This is a clear sign that the magic of the season is alive for both of them. Off they go, memories made, and now asleep in their beds as morning approaches.

But not before Mom and Dad tuck into Santa's workshop, actually my husband's workshop, for this one night each year when it is used for last-minute wrapping. A time we have come to enjoy as parents. We are organized—using a box cutter rather than scissors, an old butcher block on sawhorses for a table— and one by one we send the presents down the line. It's a process. With each present wrapped to perfection, we place them gently around the tree. Ahhh. We await those glorious surprised faces when the children awake.

Having our Christmases in the mountains is great, but it occasionally poses some challenges. This past Christmas Eve, after John had gone to bed, I went back down to the workshop (I have to confess that I rarely venture there other than at Christmas). I was finishing up the last few gifts as a substantial winter storm moved in. Above the sound of Christmas music I could hear the wind and rain pelting the windows upstairs. I was sorry that it wasn't snow but was happy that we were safe and warm in our home. I assured myself that we had prepared for this and didn't have to travel, so no worries. In similar conditions trees regularly come down along the road and knock out the electricity. Being at the end of the line as we are, it can take a while for the utility company to restore power. So in an effort to be better safe than sorry we had installed a backup generator capable of providing power to the whole house. It was a big investment, but it had already come in handy a few times and I had come to rely on it. . . .

The next thing I knew, the lights began to flicker . . . and then I got plunged into complete darkness. No flashlight handy, but why should I care? The generator would fire up in, Three. Two. One.

Nothing.

No lights.

No generator humming.

"What is happening?"

It was pitch-black down there. I literally couldn't see my hand in front of my face. I was worried that if I moved I would bump into a giant saw blade or knock something over. But I had no choice. I had to stagger around and feel my way out of the room. As I did, a conversation with the man who'd sold us the generator kept running through my head. When I asked the owner of the company what to do if the generator should ever fail to work, he said, "Call me." I shook his hand and said, "Then that's what I'll do."

And that's exactly what I did on that cold, dark, very early Christmas morning. After I finally reached him and explained our situation, there was a short pause before he said, "Let me get a cup of coffee and I'll be right over." And that he did.

In the meantime, the kids woke and were into their stockings. We couldn't wait any longer for Christmas. We got out the flashlights, lit candles, and opened the gifts without a single light illuminated on the tree. It wasn't quite the same as a candlelight vigil at the church, but it's a story that I'll tell for many, many years. The sound of the generator finally kicking on was music to my ears. At the end of the day, we had a very merry Christmas, and the memories of the kids opening gifts by flashlight are among some of my all-time favorites.

From the eyes of a seven-year-old girl to a young reporter on the beat and now to a mother seeing Christmas through the eyes of her young children, my perspective has changed dramatically over the years. But there has always been one constant: the magic. The magic of the holidays and the importance of keeping the Christmas spirit alive.

Sandra Smith serves as the coanchor of *America Reports* (weekdays 1–3 p.m. ET).

Charles Payne

Charles Payne's happy Christmases are due to the kind of care
and devotion that he received from his mom and from family.
Those elements, he reminds us, are the basic ingredients of
success, and it's important to remember this with gratitude.

For me, memories of Christmas are wrapped up in thoughts of my beloved mother. She was the greatest gift I ever received in my life. So Christmas thoughts are Mom thoughts. Even though she passed away four years ago, she's still a powerful and welcome presence in our lives. That's what a mom does for us. She brings us into the world, and no matter what happens down the line, she stays with us in one form or another. We talk about gifts that keep on giving,

From left: Clarence, Ruth holding Cecil, and Charles Payne.

well, that's what my mom is to me, and I try to emulate her and follow her example the best that I can at Christmas and all year round.

It isn't easy being married to a man who serves his country in the military. I don't think I realized this until much later, but having to pick up and move nearly every year, having to be the lone parent when your spouse is deployed and you're separated by miles and time zones, none of that is easy. Yet as a kid I didn't think much about how different my childhood was from so many others'.

I just lived my life and enjoyed it, thanks to all the sacrifices my parents made for us.

In a way, I had two childhoods. The first was when we were the typical nuclear family—my mom and dad, my two younger brothers, and me. We spent time in New York, then in Pennsylvania, Texas, Alabama, North Carolina, and Virginia. Add in time in Germany and Japan, and you've got a lot of moving and switching schools and things by the time I was twelve. Truth is, I thought of it as an ideal life. We often lived on army bases, and so, even overseas, we had your typical idyllic Christmas. Base housing was tranquil, manicured, safe, and pleasant. Mostly though, we lived in off-base housing, and even there we experienced a real sense of community. Neighbors looked out for neighbors, especially if a family had been separated due to an assignment. Every Christmas I had was really happy and joyous thanks to my mom and my dad. I know that military personnel don't earn as much as they deserve to, but Mom and Dad always made sure that, come Christmas especially, we never went without—far from it. I realize now, as an adult, just how much my mom and dad did for us. I was grateful back then, but I really understand and appreciate their efforts even more so now.

My father wasn't around as often as my mom was. He had to go to work and sometimes he was deployed and away from home for months. Still, when he was there, he was the kind of father every kid hopes for.

My siblings and I were like most kids. We couldn't wait to open our gifts, and despite orders to the contrary, we'd get up earlier than my parents would have liked. They were okay with us getting up at four or five in the morning. I can recall times when I heard my dad up on Christmas Eve assembling things for us to open the next morning. It must have been tough for Mom and Dad to get up that early, but they would do anything for their kids.

Christmas on a military base was like Christmas most everywhere, no matter what part of the United States or what country we were in. There were decorations inside and outside the housing units, Christmas parties, and a sense of goodwill and the spirit of the season spread around the base. I don't think that one of my favorite Christmas gifts, plastic posed army men (the guy with the flamethrower was my favorite), made me any different from any other young child who glamorized war and heroism.

I wouldn't learn this until later, but the reality of war in part caused the end of that "goodwill and peace among men" childhood experience. My dad came up to me at my mom's funeral, decades after they'd been divorced, and explained that he had gone out on a couple of operations while serving in Vietnam. Twice he went out and he was the only one from his unit to return alive. He believed that God had cursed him. He'd had his best friends, his brothers-in-arms, taken away from him. He was never the same after that, and it was not long thereafter when my family, that tight-knit unit, fell apart. Thanks to my mom, the four us, she and us kids, didn't just survive their separation and divorce, we eventually thrived. It would be a lot of years before I ever heard from Dad again after Mom loaded us up in the car and drove us from the US Army Garrison in Fort Lee to Harlem. We didn't just change zip codes; we traded a way of life. Gone was the neatly trimmed lawn. Gone were the separate bedrooms, kitchen, and living area. We moved into a one-room apartment in what was, in the early 1970s, one of the most dangerous urban areas in America.

That had to have been tough for my mom, being so far away from family and her roots in Alabama. But she managed—more than managed. She worked herself to the bone and made sure that she continued to help us stay on the right path that we'd started down when it was all of us together. Even though I loved those army men and an electronic football game I got another year for Christmas, my favorite gift ever was an unlikely one for a teenage boy. The year before the family split up, I'd gotten a desk and a chemistry set for Christmas. I was very happy with those "brainy gifts." The year after the split, for some reason that I can't quite remember but which seems aspirational now, I wanted a briefcase. I hoped, and I hoped, and I hoped, and on Christmas Day, Mom didn't disappoint

me. She wasn't making much money and Christmas was nowhere near what it had been in years before, but I got that briefcase. I'll never forget the sound of it clicking open and the surprise I experienced when I saw that Mom had gone overboard and put a calculator in there too!

I was set!

Paying for college was going to be difficult, so I enlisted in the air force and eventually got my degree. After that I found myself back in Harlem, living the kind of hand-to-mouth existence I had with my mom and brothers. We had a tiny room. I'd gotten married in Guam and had a two-month-old daughter, and we slept on a pull-out couch. We ate a lot, and I mean a lot, of ramen noodles. I had watched my mom working so hard and pursuing every opportunity she could, so I followed her lead and wasn't afraid of taking chances and knocking on doors. I got a job working at EF Hutton, a brokerage firm, and it was amazing to be making thirteen thousand dollars a year. Mom taught us that you can always rely on family, and that you should, so we moved out of that tiny room in Harlem to share an apartment with my brother. It was a better part of Harlem, though still rough, and I waged war against the rats there, and we suffered our losses against them.

For years I worked hard and rose up through the ranks, switched jobs, and altered directions, but I always felt like there was light guiding me and blessing me. I've been fortunate, very fortunate, that my mom set that example for me. She was always a deeply religious woman, the daughter of a Baptist preacher. In time she converted to become a Jehovah's Witness. They don't celebrate Christmas, but despite that Mom would drive up from Alabama to celebrate with all her kids and her grandkids. She knew how important it was to the rest of us. She also knew that without her sweet potato pie and her pecan pie and all the other good food she whipped up (like banana pudding with vanilla wafers), Christmas would not be complete. We had some wonderful, some huge, some spectacular Christmases with her before she passed. I was pleased to have done well enough in life to buy her a home she really liked back in Uniontown, Alabama, her hometown. When she was growing up, she wouldn't have been able to live in the part of town where that house sits. If she were a servant she would have been able to work there, but she couldn't have lived there. She moved into the former mayor's house, and to see her, retired and happy, living in a place that showed signs of progress, and being able to help her get that as a way to thank her for all she'd done for my brothers and me, that was really, really special. Still, after she passed, I wished I had done more for her. I'd let her know she was loved and appreciated, but she'd done so much more for me than I could ever do for her.

As much as I love Christmas and all that goes with it—I'm a grandfather now and get to distribute gifts like I did when I was a dad and really love it, and as much as I love listening to Nat King Cole singing "The Christmas Song" or Stevie Wonder doing his version of "The Little Drummer Boy"—it's another kind of giving and receiving that makes the season so important and wonderful. I've been fortunate in my career and in my personal life. I'm blessed with great kids and grandchildren, but my wife received one of the greatest gifts possible. She has had a very serious heart condition since she was a teenager. Doctors had tried numerous treatments, she'd undergone multiple procedures, and she was finally at a point when nothing was working as they hoped. It seemed as if her death was imminent.

I was filling in for Stuart Varney on FOX, and during a commercial break, I noticed that I had received an email from a close friend. He was living in California then, and his daughter had died. I was stunned and saddened. He was reaching out because he wanted my wife to receive his daughter's heart. I wasn't sure how to respond to his kindness. I forwarded the message to my wife and finished up the show. There were a lot of obstacles to overcome. Normally hearts can't be transported more than four hours; that and other things made the possibility of a transplant seem like a real, real long shot if not a hopeless case. (I was forgetting my mom's example—she always believed that things would work out.) A day later, my wife called, excited and crying. She'd been approved for the heart transplant; if we could get out to Los Angeles, she'd receive it. I went to the daughter's funeral while there. It was devastating. She was only twenty-one years old, but she had the forethought at that age to sign up as an organ donor. She was thinking of others and not just herself.

And speaking of moms, my wife and the mother of the young woman who died are now best friends. My second-oldest granddaughter is named after the donor. That young woman gave us back my wife, my kids' mom, their kids' grandmother. I don't know how to describe how grateful we are. That word feels inadequate, and it seemed like there was no way to say anything or do anything to thank my friend's family. But, of course, there was. There is always something you can do, and in this case, it took the form of paying it forward. What better way to honor their daughter than to give in a new way?

I'd heard of other people doing this, so I make no claim on originality here, but the intent is what matters. For the past nine years since my wife's recovery, we've gone to various stores at different times in the LA and New York/New Jersey areas, found the layaway department, and asked people if we could help them out by paying off what they owed on purchases they were in the process of making. We supplement that with other items they need. We give them some additional cash to help them.

The first time we did that, when we were in Los Angeles, I was so overcome with emotion when I saw their response to us, how grateful they were. I kept thinking, "You have no idea what we've been given, all the blessings we've received." I was so worked up. I was crying my eyes out. I had to walk away. I didn't want to draw attention to myself. My wife stayed and continued to do those good works. On top of the gratitude I was feeling for my wife having had her health restored, I was also responding to the memories I had from my childhood. I remember my mom putting items on layaway. I knew it was stressful for her. It was a good service the stores were offering, but the closer you got to Christmas, the more you had to watch your pennies! It was a countdown to Christmas, and you wanted to be sure you could pay for the item so that you could present it as a gift and put it under the tree. Making sure your kids didn't wind up wondering why they had to do without when others had so much more was important to my mom and later on to me. There were enough things going on telling you that you were less than that adding one more would be heartbreaking.

In the vast majority of cases, I'd say 99 percent of the recipients are single moms. We've got a soft spot in our hearts for anyone in need, but given the situation my mom had to deal with, there's a special section of our hearts reserved for women like her who find themselves in tough circumstances.

Even before this, my family and I had tried to do what we could to lift up people in need. We'd been generous to the community and to our family, just as my mom was. Convent Baptist Church in Harlem played a crucial role in my life after my mom and my brothers moved to that section of the city. I could have gone a different way in life without the influence of the ministering that was done there. One year, to make sure that other kids got the opportunity that I did, my wife and I donated fifty backpacks (I got vetoed on the idea of donating briefcases!) and loaded them with books and supplies. One child who received one of those told the people at the church that that gift changed his life. He'd been led to believe that he didn't matter to anyone outside his own family. Such a simple gesture like that changed a life.

We extend our generosity beyond Christmas to hosting parties throughout the year. One of them is an Easter egg hunt where we have kids from the neighborhood over and reward them with cash and gifts to aid their education, like computer tablets. I started with a humble calculator thanks to my mom; imagine how far a kid can go with the technology available today? So, showing kids some love, some interest, some concern for their future? That's all because people did those things for me.

At the top of my wish list for everyone is that they can experience the kind of care and devotion that I received from my mom and from my family. Those are the basic ingredients of success. Add the kind of perseverance in the face of obstacles I witnessed as my mom did everything in her power to make sure that if part one of my life was great and part two was tough but manageable, then I had everything I needed and wanted to contribute to my family's legacy. I'll tell you, I still walk around my house and I'm in awe when I think of the part so many people played in my story. It's having a happy ending too. As each year comes to a close and Christmas is near, I'm reminded of that. We all have a role we play in helping one another to get the most out of the time we have. I miss my mom so much, but I also know she's here and she still enjoys seeing her kin making the most of the gift she gave us—hope for a better tomorrow.

Charles Payne is the host of FOX Business Network's *Making Money with Charles Payne* (weekdays 2–3 p.m. ET).

John Rich

Giving, for John Rich, is the ultimate spirit of Christmas.
Sometimes you give; sometimes you make a sacrifice to
people you love and people you care about. John received a
gift from his father that changed the course of his life.

One Christmas, with a single gift, my dad pretty much changed the direction of my life. I grew up in Amarillo, which is up in the panhandle of Texas. It's flat as a board, and the wind blows forty miles an hour on a calm day. We got horrific tornadoes on account of it being located in Tornado Alley. My Granny Rich is from about ninety minutes east of there in Pampa, Texas. So I've got a lot of deep roots out in Texas.

My dad started preaching at nineteen years old, but he was not the kind of

John Rich brings Christmas cheer to The Greg Gutfeld Show.

preacher that preached in the big churches. He was more of a prison ministry preacher. He did a lot of revivals, he still does, and did so all through his youth. He would go to events like Mardi Gras and stand on the corner with a guitar around his neck singing gospel music and preaching to people as they walked by. That was his calling in life. So he was very good at it and had a lot of success. He got a lot of people to consider eternity, people who wouldn't ever have walked into a church building. They got to hear the truth coming from my dad, so that was his mission in life.

Well, he was involved in a great mission, but it didn't pay well. And so to support himself at first, and later his family, my dad did every kind of job you can imagine. I watched him slop hogs in a hog barn down the road from where we lived. He sold cars. He gave guitar lessons. He was the night watchman at Amarillo National Bank. There were times when he would work more than a hundred hours a week to provide for us all. He did an amazing job of that, and he set a great example for us. He had his calling; he had his day job; he made it all work so that we never wanted for anything.

When I was about five or six years old, he said, "Hey, you want to go with me to watch me teach guitar lessons?"

I said, "Sure." What kid doesn't want to tag along with his dad? So we headed out to the music store in Amarillo where he taught. I went down there and took a seat behind him. I watched as he instructed fifteen-to-twenty-five-year-old people how to play guitar. There were about ten or twelve of them in the class. At one point he handed me a little plastic guitar. I think he just wanted me to have something in my hands so I didn't feel out of place. It was like I was another one of the students. I took that guitar and got started learning. Over the next year, I got to where I could take that little plastic guitar, and I could play everything his students were playing; then I got to where, for the most part, I could play everything he was playing.

By the time I was six going on seven, he invited me to sit behind him in the pulpit to play guitar. Him honoring me that way was something special. He would be standing there singing "I'll Fly Away" or "Amazing Grace," and I would be sitting down, kind of hiding behind him at the pulpit with my guitar on my knee playing along. Over time he must have started to recognize that, "Wow, my son's pretty good at this, he needs a better guitar than that." I didn't know he was thinking that. But we rolled around to Christmas and I went to open up what we called our big Christmas present. It was a big box and I sat there thinking about what it could be. I couldn't figure it out. I opened this box up and what I saw was the guitar I'd been watching my dad play since the beginning of my life. It was the guitar that he always played, the one he played at church, the one he gave lessons on, the one that was his go-to, his tool, his instrument. I was only seven, and I was looking at that guitar and then at him. At first I was wondering if this was a joke of some kind. Why would he give me the thing that he so clearly loved and used?

I didn't understand.

He understood that I didn't understand, so he said, "You're as good as I am right now on this instrument. You need a real guitar, and with it you're going to be better than I am. I have no doubt you will be better than me. So I want you to have it and use it."

At the time, even though he said that to me, I still didn't really understand. I still didn't really get it and all that gesture meant for him and for me. I now know that he had to give me his guitar because he couldn't really afford, at that point in time, to buy me my own guitar. At least not a legitimate instrument like that one was. It was a very fine piece of craftsmanship, the kind that someone could play for twenty years.

As children we don't really think about the gravity of a gesture like that. Back then I just thought, "Okay, I guess I now own my dad's guitar. That's cool. It's a really nice guitar."

But as I got older, I thought about that gift he gave me that Christmas. It was hard for me to imagine what it must have felt like for my dad to give me his guitar like that. I couldn't know the feeling, but I knew the reason. He sacrificed something that was important to him because he recognized that I had a real gift with that instrument and possibly had a future with it. He wanted to give me every benefit he could manage to give me. And even though he couldn't afford to give it to me, he had something to give that was bigger than anything money could buy. He taught me about sacrifice, about putting someone else's interests ahead of your own, about putting your faith in something that you can't see yet but you know is going to come down the line.

From that point forward, at eight years old, nine years old, fourteen years old, seventeen years old, I'd play that guitar. I don't believe I bought another guitar until I was twenty years old.

And I'll tell you what, that guitar was and is something. Back in the late sixties and early seventies, Electro-Harmonix, which made guitars for about three or four years, made rosewood guitars like the one my dad passed on to me. Those guitars rivaled what Martin made. He must have had to work pretty hard and save pretty seriously to afford it when he was about twenty or so.

I still have that guitar at my house; that's the guitar I auditioned on for bands. I played it at talent contests when I was in high school. All that ultimately led to me getting noticed by the music industry and then having a music career. It all started with him handing that off to me.

Musical instruments to a guy like me, they're living, breathing organisms. I look at that thing and I'll say to myself, "That guitar still has songs in it. It's still alive. I will never write all the songs that are living inside that instrument right there." I can pass it down to my kids and they'll never write all the songs in it either. It's a limitless thing because music is limitless. I saw in that guitar and felt in playing music that I could do whatever I set my mind to. I didn't see that at the time; I just went on playing it.

I knew his gift to me was a big thing, but it didn't dawn on me what a momentous, powerful dad thing that was until I had my own kids. That's when I realized, wow, what a thing—to give up something that had to have had so much meaning for him. I thought to myself, "What did he play after that?" About ten years ago, I had a talk with him about it. He told me he would borrow a guitar and then he took one out on layaway. I mean, he definitely was able to get his hands on a guitar, but he gave me the guitar that he loved. As a musician myself,

The beloved guitar that John Rich's father gave him.

I know that I own guitars that I would rather you take off one of my hands than take that guitar. You aren't taking it from me. I'm not going to sell it to you. You cannot have it under any circumstances. Not because of its monetary value, but because of what I've done with it. The history in that guitar, where it's been and then the music I have created on it, and what that music has done, you just don't let it go.

I knew he had the same feelings about the Electro-Harmonix, but I'm his son. He wanted it; I needed it. It was just as simple as that for him; that's the essence of being a good dad.

And so to me, that is also the ultimate spirit of Christmas. Sometimes you give; sometimes you make a sacrifice to people you love and people you care about. You're letting them know how much you think about them, how much you care about them, you let them know that there is nothing you wouldn't do for them. I have two boys now who are nine and eleven and I think about what I can give them that really isn't about how much it costs. There's another kind of "value" of things.

At Christmas and the rest of the year, I got the gifts of life lessons about the right way to live. Once I was able to afford it, I returned the favor to my dad. On his birthday, I wanted to get him something he'd always wanted. He'd often talked about how cool it would be to become a licensed pilot. So I got him some lessons. That's how it is in the Rich family; we'll give you a bump you need to get going, but it's still on you to do it.

Same is true with gifts I get for my kids. Both my sons like to play baseball and basketball. So I'll get them some of the gear that they want and need, like a really good baseball bat that some other kid on the team had and my son admired. I got the bat, and then I said, "I gave you the bat, but I can't get you a spot on the team or in the starting lineup. You got the bat from me, but I can't make you go out in the yard and swing it six hundred times in practice. That bat doesn't come with a guarantee that you're ever going to hit a home run. That's on you. So here it is."

"Thanks, Daddy."

"You got it, man. Go practice."

I think they know what I'm telling them. They watched their dad do it in real time. I don't expect anybody to give me anything. So me giving them a good tool . . . it's like my dad giving me that guitar. I think that concept is

Dana Perino meets Santa Claus!

Courtesy of Dana Perino

Jesse Watters; his sister,
Aliza; and his mom,
Anne, opening gifts.

Courtesy of Jesse Watters

Jesse's childhood obsession with
getting a Michael Jackson jacket
would finally pay off when Dana
Perino tracked it down.

Courtesy of FOX News

THE FIVE CHRISTMAS SPECIAL

Bret Baier's boys, Paul and Daniel, had been wanting a puppy for ages, so he decided to spring a Christmas surprise on them on air.

Courtesy of FOX News

Paul's time in the hospital taught the Baier family the importance of giving back, which they pour into their gift-giving drives at the holidays.

Courtesy of Bret Baier

Brit Hume and Bret Baier at a Christmas party. Brit's favorite memories include riding his bike through Washington, DC, on one snowy Christmas morning in 1953.

Courtesy of FOX News

Lawrence Jones and his mom, Tameria.
Lawrence's parents always taught him the value of hard
work, aspiration, and sacrifice.

Courtesy of Lawrence Jones

Ainsley Earhardt loves passing down Christmas
traditions to her daughter, Hayden, that she got from her
mom *(pictured)* and dad.

Courtesy of Ainsley Earhardt

Brian Kilmeade enjoys celebrating Christmas with his Great Pyrenees, Apollo *(right)* and Rocky. Below are Kilmeade brothers, Jim, Brian, and Steve, along with cousin Kevin *(seated)* and uncle Joe.

Courtesy of Amy Sohnen; courtesy of Brian Kilmeade

John Roberts loves making
Christmas memories with his
twin children, Sage and Kellan,
and wife, Kyra.

Courtesy of John Roberts

Amid the chaos, Sandra Smith remembers to be grateful for the quiet moments at Christmas with her husband, John, and kids, Cora and Johnny.

Courtesy of Julie Talarico; courtesy of Jill C. Smith Photography

Martha MacCallum and Bill Hemmer in Rockefeller Center.

Courtesy of Martha MacCallum

Shannon Bream and her husband, Sheldon, enjoy Christmas with Santa.

Courtesy of Shannon Bream

For Geraldo Rivera, finding just the right balance between his Catholic and Jewish heritages was a struggle during childhood Decembers, but the Rivera family eventually decided on a "Chrismukkah" compromise. *Pictured:* Geraldo; his wife, Erica; his sister, Sharon; his daughter, Sol; and his mother, Lil.

Courtesy of Geraldo Rivera

For the Duffy family, Christmas means everything from sledding to honoring the true meaning of the season by observing Advent to picking a tree.

Courtesy of the Duffy family and (left, center) Jessica Kopecky Design

Janice Dean often spends
Christmas at the firehouse
where her husband works.
She loves sharing those
memories with her sons,
Theodore and Matthew.

Courtesy of Janice Dean

The Doocy family loves capturing memories of Christmases past on camera. Steve's affection for Christmas cookies goes back to childhood and Sally, Kathy, and Peter enjoy carrying on the tradition!

Courtesy of the Doocy family

For Bill Hemmer, Christmas wouldn't be Christmas
without being at home with family. *From left:* Charlie the dog,
Ann, Bill, Andy, Tracy, and Kris *(seated).*

Courtesy of Bill Hemmer

Maria Bartiromo has fond memories of Christmases
in her family's restaurant, the best Italian place in Brooklyn,
and her dad's amazing pizza. *Pictured below:* Maria with older
siblings, Theresa and Patrick, and mother, Josephine.

Courtesy of Maria Bartiromo

Emily Compagno loves Christmas, from assembling
nativity sets to dancing in *The Nutcracker.*

Courtesy of Emily Compagno

everything. You don't want to give your kids an advantage, that's not going to help them to go build something with it. Encourage them to go work, to build something great. That's a concept that I live by even today.

I got that gift, that understanding about the naure of work, from watching my Granny Rich. If you ask Granny Rich, "Why are you still working at eighty-eight years old?" She'll look at you with pretty much a scowl on her face. She'll eye you up, looking through the smoke of a lit cigarette, and say, "Because I can. That's what you're supposed to do when you live in this country." Her generation didn't believe in not producing, not being worth something, not bringing something to the table. Whatever you can do, do it. Do it as long as you're able to do it. And that's what America is built on.

I'm very fortunate to have grown up around people like Granny Rich and her generation. Witnessing firsthand as they aged, I still see the fire in their eyes. I still hear their jokes and laugh with them. I still watch them having fun. They're still engaged with life, still have opinions to express, still look forward to waking up every morning.

I want to be like them.

What does that mean?

I go at life like they went at life. They didn't waste any time. I don't waste any time.

Granny Rich would always say that our country doesn't guarantee you the right to be happy; it guarantees you the right to pursue happiness. I didn't have the right to expect my dad to hand over that guitar to me. He wasn't giving me a guarantee when he did it; he was asking me to promise him that I'd make the most of an opportunity I'd earned.

That's the spirit we would celebrate with our redneck all American Christmases. For so many years, we'd all go to Granny Rich's house. She and my granddaddy Papa Rich—a World War II vet with six Purple Hearts who's one of the toughest dudes you will ever meet—would host us all. We'd show up at

Granny's house, and she didn't roast turkeys like a lot of folks do; she fried chickens. And when I say chickens, I mean five or six of them. For our Christmas meal, we'd have platters of fried chicken, battalions of mashed potatoes, everything you could possibly eat times ten. We got the whole family together; they drove in from all over the place. We'd settle into our seats and my dad would pray over the food, a revival-style prayer. We could feel the energy humming through the house.

When the bones were all picked clean, Pap would say, "Well, you guys ready to go shooting?"

Everybody would jump up from the table, grab a cup of coffee, and walk out onto the back porch. We'd all have a shotgun and here we'd go! My granddaddy would launch skeet off the back porch, and we'd be blasting away at those clay targets. Granny'd be inside smoking a cigarette, watching the news.

That was Christmas with the Riches, which was just incredible. When you grow up with veterans, and you grow up with preachers, and you grow up with musicians, and you celebrate with strong ladies who survived the Dust Bowl days and who still run their own businesses and sip a little whiskey and smoke cigarettes till they're almost ninety, you know that you're with family. That's our Christmas.

John Rich is the host of *The Pursuit! with John Rich* on FOX Nation, as well as a country music singer and songwriter.

The
Joy of
Faith

Martha MacCallum

Martha MacCallum reflects on her childhood faith, the
way Christmas offers hope to a divided nation, and why
it's vital to remember "what Christmas is all about."

A few years ago, I ordered a "Keep Christ in Christmas" magnet for our car. It may seem to some like an obnoxious thing to put on your car, but it really wasn't a message for others; it was for me. It was so that every time I got in my car or put something in the trunk, I would see it. And it would remind me about the baby and the manger, instead of the packages in my arms and the list in my pocket.

I have always loved Christmas. Literally almost everything about it.

For Martha MacCallum (right), much of Christmas centers on religious traditions, but it's also focused on family, such as memories of her sisters, Lisa (left) and Jane (middle).

As a child I would say "merry Christmas" to everyone, everywhere I went. I liked saying it and I liked seeing people's reactions. I still do. But as I got older, and as I grew more firm in my Roman Catholic beliefs, it became more and more important to me to try to remember each step of the way what it's really all about. It's like Linus says in *A Charlie Brown Christmas*: "I can tell you what Christmas is all about." He asks someone to turn on a spotlight. He then launches into

Luke's Gospel of the Nativity story. "The angel of the Lord came upon them, and the glory of the Lord shone round about them, and they were sore afraid . . ." Now he's got all his unruly friends' attention, and they listen, rapt, to the true meaning of Christmas.

Keeping that true meaning the focus is important, and that influences the sort of traditions I've embraced around celebrating Christmas. For me, Christmas begins not with store decorations that seem to nudge Halloween off the shelves these days, or the Black Friday sales, but on the first Sunday of Advent. That is "go" day for the season at our house. We put a fresh green wreath on the dinner table with three purple candles and one pink, light the first one, and say an Advent prayer. Each year I buy old-school German Advent calendars and send a few to family members or the kids at college and keep one for our kitchen. I still delight in opening the little windows and the way that it paces the season, keeping each day special. Those larger doors with the "24" on them hold the magic of Christmas Eve.

A few years ago, in a nod to the omnipresence of social media in everyone's lives, I started to post an Advent calendar. Each day I look for something that reminds me that we are "waiting," that everyone is preparing by decorating and shopping and wrapping and singing and praying and that all these things light the candle of what's to come in our hearts as we anticipate the birth of Christ. The Rockefeller Center tree going up just after Thanksgiving, a child looking in the window of FAO Schwarz, a drippy iced gingerbread house, an angel on my tree, the wreaths that line St. Patrick's Cathedral, the empty manger bed in the crèche there, waiting for the baby Jesus. All of these are photos that I stop to take. They make me appreciate the day, the effort that goes into all of these Christmas things, and the reason for it all. Sometimes I post a prayer, like the Christmas novena, which my mother-in-law always said at the table on Christmas Eve. A tradition we have kept going.

In our home, I put out my collection of crèches. One small one was made with wood from the Holy Land; another one so tiny you can hold it in your hand is made in Columbia from a matchbox. It's painted with bright and beautiful colors. The one my mom bought for us when we were married is from Italy, with beautiful carved figures. Again, we keep Jesus in a secret hiding place until after midnight on Christmas Eve.

There is a beautiful drama to the Christmas story. The shepherds keeping watch, the Wise Men on their way, believing what the prophets foretold. The ability of Mary, a young woman, to have such faith, that God was with her. As Amy Grant sings in one of my favorite newer carols, and the only one I know that speaks in the voice of Mary, "Breath of Heaven," "Holy Father you have come, and chosen me now to carry your son."

The song is about Mary's awe at what's been asked of her. It lays bare her fear, her soul, and her plaintive plea that the breath of heaven come to her aid; it is a prayer to God above, one that we can all identify with at various times in our lives: "Be with me now. Be with me now."

My daughter, Elizabeth, and her friends sang this song every Christmas in the choir at Oak Knoll School of the Holy Child. It was a highlight of those years, and still today if I can coax it out of them, they sing it for us again around the piano at home.

The Virgin Mary is a central figure in the drama of the Christmas story. The angel Gabriel told her of God's mission for her. She was chosen by God to carry His Son. She was with Him on His journey that would lead to His death at just thirty-three. That journey began with her "full of grace" and "blessed is the fruit of thy womb, Jesus." She was a teenager in Nazareth, engaged to be married, but pregnant already. Hers was a burden that could break anyone, incense any parent, and certainly cause any fiancé to flee. But not Joseph. He too was visited. This frightened, and no doubt angry, young man was told as well, "Do not be afraid. . . . What is conceived in her is from the Holy Spirit. She will give birth to a Son and you are to give Him the name Jesus." Mary and Joseph, how did they have such faith in the face of all the reasons not to believe? Imagine them as your children, real people—who would believe their story? An immaculate conception by the Holy Spirit? Imagine the looks, the scorn, the gossip. Imagine the love and faith it took to overcome it. That kind of faith could change the world, and it did.

"Ave Maria" is among my most favorite songs to hear at Christmas. My mother sang in our church choir, and she loved to sing "Ave Maria." It has moving, simple Hail Mary lyrics, set to music by Franz Schubert. Sung by everyone from Pavarotti to Celine Dion, it stirs the soul and can bring tears to my eyes as I imagine Mary, heavy with child and no doubt pining for her home and bed, instead en route to Bethlehem on the back of a small donkey, led by Joseph. Can you put yourself in her place? So uncomfortable and exhausted, so far from her parents, so young and, oh yes, carrying a baby put in her belly by God?

We say, Hail Mary, full of grace . . . but how is grace defined in our lives? Grace is felt and understood more than it is defined or quantified. We know it when we feel it. You know, in your heart, when you are the beneficiary of that marriage of relief and love. You feel unworthy of all the grace given to you in life, even in the hard times. As a mother, at Christmas, and all the rest of the time, it is what you want for your children. You want them to know that they are in God's grace. Ultimately, that's the story the mass tells, that's the beginning of the full story of Jesus, what his Nativity and Christmas prefigures. So in preparing for Christmas at Advent, in taking a moment each day to open a window in an Advent calendar, we're taking the time to reflect on the immensity of God's love. We sometimes may feel like God's grace is absent, or that we are too busy to notice it. That is the message of the magnet. Keep Christ in Christmas, folks. He's there whether you realize it or not.

I lost my mother almost eight years ago. She was the center of Christmas for us all. We lost her too soon and my dad and my sisters and I miss her every day. She was a beautiful lady who carried herself with dignity and showered us with love. Even battling cancer, she wanted to know about you. What was new? How were the kids? She was a tireless optimist and her faith was quiet but omnipresent.

Her support of us, unwavering. She didn't wear her faith on her sleeve, or talk about right and wrong. She led by example. She showed you what she wanted you to know, just by the way she lived her life and how she treated others. She was fun and led with her lovely smile. She was joyous in her love for her family, her embrace of each person's unique strengths. And she knew how to do Christmas!

Both my parents were only children, so at Christmas, my sisters and I were fortunate to have all four grandparents at our house. My mother would always make it a beautiful day. When everyone arrived with packages and bags of wrapped and bowed gifts, Christmas records were playing and nuts and cheeses and shrimp with cocktail sauce were set out, Christmas cocktail napkins at the ready to catch the excess horseradishy sauce I'd laden my shrimp with. Champagne and wine for all, except the little ones, as the first presents were opened.

Then Mom would slip away and pull on her linen apron, with the embroidered Christmas candle on the front. It was perfectly pressed and ready for the big day. Her favorite Christmas dinner to prepare was first a citrus salad, with pomegranate seeds and champagne dressing, followed by a yummy and special filet mignon with a red wine sauce and cheesy potatoes au gratin. All the while relatives chatted away at the table or paused to open their "table gift." Mom always placed one last little gift on everyone's plate, wrapped in gold paper with a gold bow. Just when you thought the opening was over, there was that one more thing. Usually it was something practical in nature, a small umbrella, a bottle opener, hand cream, or a picture frame.

Then for dessert, often it was a big glass bowl filled with her fabulous chocolate mousse. It was chocolatey goodness, whipped with cream and small bits of bittersweet chocolate folded in.

Now we carry on her traditions with our own families. My husband and I make Mom's Christmas dinner, almost exactly as she did. I'm lucky that my husband, Dan, is an excellent cook! Some things evolve, but many stay the same. Now the younger generation pitches in, making desserts and helping with the dishes. I wear

Mom's Christmas candle apron. The table gift has evolved into a "Yankee swap" where each person brings a gift to put in the middle of the table. The trading gets raucous and my dad's gift is generally the one that everyone wants to steal!

Mom loved to play the piano and sing carols (her favorite was "O Holy Night"), and I have tried to keep that love alive with my children as well. When I was ten or eleven, my girlfriends and I would pick a school night to head out after our home-work was done and go caroling in our neighborhood. This was a rather messy, unorganized affair; a neat and orderly candlelit procession with leather-bound songbooks, it was not. Actually it was more like Halloween—with us running around the neighborhood and getting up the courage to ring a doorbell and just start singing. In truth, at some houses, they just turned off the lights and hoped we would go away—they weren't sure what was happening! But inevitably, some gracious neighbors were charmed by the sounds of a handful of ten-year-olds singing their lungs out in hats and mittens at their doors. They would gather around the open door and clap for us. The really nice ones would offer us a hot chocolate or candy cane for the road.

So because I had such good memories of this, I of course wanted to get my kids to do it as well. It started with my daughter, Elizabeth, and a few of her friends. A few other moms and I would walk them around the neighborhood and encourage them to run up the lawn and start singing. I realize this is a bit of a lost art and not everyone knows what's happening when someone is singing at their door, but I remember it happening occasionally when I was a child, and the sound of the voices outside when I was doing homework or watching TV filled me with so much excitement. I would run to the door and be bursting with Christmas spirit, so I've made it something of a personal mission to keep caroling alive and well!

As it turned out, these initially shy girls became very enthusiastic carolers, and each year the event grew bigger. The boys and their friends wanted to come along. (What's better than little boys throwing their heads back and singing "Hark! The Herald Angels Sing" at the top of their lungs? I ask you.)

It also turned into something of a post-caroling party. The moms and then the dads would end up coming back to our house for a bit of adult Christmas cheer, of course. Eventually they loaded the exhausted kids into their cars and took them home.

One year, I swear we had about fifty kids and twenty moms bundled up and heading out to regale the neighbors with verses of "Deck the Halls" and "Silent Night." What we didn't realize was that the snowfall and a slight temperature drop the night before had covered all the hilly front lawns with a hard, slippery, icy coating. The sidewalks weren't much better. Before we knew it the kids were slipping and sliding down the hillsides, knocking one another over and laughing all the way. The altos crashed into the sopranos and tumbled into a harmonic heap, breaking through the hard crust. The moms turned into octopuses, and like superheroes we caught little ones, preventing them from sliding into the street. After an hour or two of kid-catching and holding our breath, we realized we were just lucky everyone was still in one piece, and we packed it in and headed home for cookies and cocoa, and something stiffer for the moms!

From that year on, we took the party inside around our piano. I set up a snow village on the top, and the kids would sing and the little ones would gaze at the skaters on the mini ice rink at eye level. We had songbooks printed and bound and added the dads to the group; they brought with them some surprisingly good altos, and one or two impressed with some third-verse knowledge of "Good King Wenceslas." Our boys grew up playing football, lacrosse, and hockey, and I loved seeing the sideline dads swapping their playbooks for caroling books, chiming in with song requests, and bellowing the deep chords of "I Heard the Bells on Christmas Day." That song is a particular favorite of mine. The lyrics of the song are a poem written by Henry Wadsworth Longfellow during the Civil War, in the wake of the tragic death of his wife and the severe wounding of his son, who was an officer in the Union Army. The poem captures the haunting desperation of the nation torn apart, but signals the hope heard in the bells.

It was as if an earthquake rent
The hearth-stones of a continent,
And made forlorn
The households born
Of peace on earth, good-will to men!

And in despair I bowed my head;
"There is no peace on earth," I said;
"For hate is strong,
And mocks the song
Of peace on earth, good-will to men!"

Then pealed the bells more loud and deep:
"God is not dead; nor doth he sleep!
The Wrong shall fail,
The Right prevail,
With peace on earth, good-will to men."

It's a beautiful reminder of how, even when our nation seemed irreconcilably divided, the hope of Christmas testified to the certainty of future peace. And I remember that every time I hear it sung by carolers.

I have such fond memories of the tough little boys in our group, who with only a bit of encouragement stood shoulder to shoulder belting out tunes and

laughing. The girls were always up front, tussling over which song they wanted to sing next. Rushing through the final verse to get to the next one they couldn't wait to start.

Over time, for the kids, and for some of the adults, our singing became the sidebar to the party. Teenagers wandered off in clusters and parents chatted and laughed by the bar, nibbling on hors d'oeuvres. I became the "carol coraller"—exhorting them all to the piano, and sometimes even grabbing an elbow or a drink and tempting folks closer to the piano. Once back by the pounding keys, though, year after year, it's the part of the party that everyone loves. Someday, I hope there will be more little children around the piano, and my kids will be the ones encouraging them to sing. That is my secret plot, to create future generations of caroling nuts like me. To leave the world just a bit more Christmassy than I found it would be quite satisfying.

Not only do members of my family know their carols; we are also deeply steeped in the finer points of classic Christmas movies. Thanksgiving night usually kicks off the film festival, with *Elf*, as we joyfully recite the words before they come out of the actors' mouths: "It's a crappy cup of coffee?" And, "I like smiling; smiling's my favorite," or "SANTA'S COMING!!!"

My husband, Dan, is a big fan of Alastair Sim's *A Christmas Carol*. The old 1951 black-and-white version of Scrooge's timeless lesson brings out the sentimental side of us all—"Can you forgive a pig-headed old fool for having no eyes to see with nor ears to hear with all these years?" He also passed along the tradition from his family of watching Gian Carlo Menotti's *Amahl and the Night Visitors*, an opera about a poor little boy with a bad leg. He and his mother are visited by the Three Kings, who are on their way to see the baby Jesus, and a miracle happens along the way.

Which brings us full circle to Linus and the moment my kids watched over and over in their pajamas as little children, and still manage to curl up for once during the season all these years later:

"For unto you is born this day in the City of David a Savior, which is Christ the Lord. And this shall be a sign unto you. Ye shall find the babe wrapped in swaddling clothes, lying in a manger. . . ."

Merry Christmas to all, and to all a good night!

Martha MacCallum currently serves as the anchor and executive editor of *The Story with Martha MacCallum* (weekdays, 3–4 p.m. ET).

Shannon Bream

*Shannon Bream has lots of happy Christmas memories but keeps in mind
that the holiday serves as a reminder of God's light in the darkest of times.*

There are a lot of serious reasons to love Christmas. It's the time we celebrate the birth of Jesus, the first appearance in history of the incarnate God! But for me, a slightly less serious one is that Jesus and I nearly share a birthday.

I'm not a Christmas baby, but if I'd decided to delay my entrance into the world by forty-eight hours or so, I would have been. Having a birthday on December 23 isn't as bad as it might sound. Yes, everyone is very excited about Christmas and looking forward to it, but I never felt like my birthday got overlooked as a result. And who can resent Christmas, especially when your par-

Shannon Bream doesn't confine her enjoyment of Christmas music to November through December.

ents give you the middle name Noelle in honor of that amazing holiday? And who can complain about the festive season when you're sent home from the hospital on Christmas Day and you're bundled up in a red stocking? As a result of this twin pairing of birthday and Christmas, December is my favorite, favorite time of year. How many kids can say that they never had to go to school on their birthday? How many kids can say that they had two special days in that short of a span?

If there's one downside to this, and it eventually turned out to be an upside as well, it's that my parents divorced when I was only a year old. I have no memories of them being together, so my earliest recollections are of spending my two big days with each separately. Divorce is a sad event in any kid's life, but for me, I got to enjoy double celebrations of my birthday and Christmas each year. That helped offset the pain of their splitting up. Whether I was with Mom or Dad on Christmas or my birthday was a matter of them agreeing to a plan. That arrangement varied, but in my adult life, there's been one Christmas event that I can always count on.

For the last fifty-plus years, until the coronavirus interrupted the tradition, my husband's aunt Dink has hosted a family gathering on Christmas Eve. We attend every other year. Aunt Dink (her actual name is Arietta, but I don't know anyone who calls her that) is an absolute marvel. She takes Christmas to a whole new level every year. She's one of the kindest and most talented women I know. She decorates her house for weeks and weeks. Many of her treasures are ceramics she created with her own hands. She has other collections that date back decades. She's a wonderful hostess, and we love attending church on Christmas Eve and then going to her place. We're a large group crammed into her house among the decorations that light up, move, and play music. They occupy rooms and rooms, and it's just a gorgeous, festive place to be. If you've ever seen the window decorations at Saks Fifth Avenue or another Manhattan department store, then you've seen the quality and variety of what Aunt Dink is able to produce.

Aunt Joan's Secret Christmas Punch

(No wonder we love it—look at all that sugar!)

Serves 50–60 people

9½ ounces (1 cup) powdered cherry Kool-Aid
2 gallons Hawaiian Punch
Two 46-ounce cans pineapple juice
Three 6-ounce cans frozen concentrated orange juice
2 liters ginger ale, plus more if needed
2 cups sugar

Place the Kool-Aid powder in a large freezer-safe bowl or container and add enough water to dissolve the Kool-Aid. Add the Hawaiian Punch, pineapple juice, orange juice, ginger ale, and sugar and stir until the frozen orange juice is dissolved. Taste and add more sugar and/or ginger ale as needed. Place in freezer and stir frequently to keep the mixture from separating until it reaches a "slushy" consistency. Serve immediately.

That party wouldn't be complete without Santa Claus dropping by to deliver presents for the kids. He arrives shortly after I've had my first cup of Aunt Joan's delicious, nonalcoholic punch. I'm usually the first one at the punch bowl, having waited not so patiently for its arrival. I worked on getting the recipe for twenty-five-plus years! While I'm sipping away, there's a knock at the door and Santa comes in with a bag slung over his shoulder. He emits a jolly, "Ho, ho, ho," before taking a seat while the kids gather around him. By this time, the adults have been scanning the room, trying to figure out on whom Aunt Dink bestowed the honor of playing Santa for the kids. My husband has spent a considerable amount of time over the years trying to determine the secret recipe of the selection process Aunt Dink uses to make her choice. For him, one ingredient he would add to the list is this—frustration. He was nearing fifty years old and he'd never gotten to play Santa.

To be honest, if having a Santa-like physique is part of the equation, then I can understand why Aunt Dink hadn't yet selected him. Sheldon is an angular six feet three inches tall, and he weighs 195 pounds. I can't say that he grew into the rotund role and that's why he was selected, but the look of delight on his face when Aunt Dink made the call notifying him of his selection was as satisfying to see as Aunt Joan's punch is to drink. As part of the honor, he had to don the Santa suit, complete with the belly pillow. This one-size-has-to-fit-all suit has been used for years and years and is a bit threadbare in spots, but he managed to look good in it and executed his job well. Santa calls out the names of all the kids one by one. They come up and sit on his lap and he presents each of them with a gift. Sheldon went a little off script, calling me up for a special presentation. I sat on his lap and he gave me a kiss that crossed the boundary between a quick peck and a passionate smooch. The kids lost their minds when they all saw Aunt Shannon kissing Santa Claus. I don't know how many of them thought of the classic song, but I sure did. If the kids were to write their version, it would be, based on what they were shouting, "Santa Was Making Out with Aunt Shannon!"

Another constant in my Christmas life was the presence of my maternal grandparents: Nell and Phil. Actually, they were a fixture in my life throughout the year. After the divorce, Mom and I moved in with them in Florida. One of the memories I treasure is going with them to the Diplomat hotel in Hollywood, Florida. There we'd have a Christmas Day brunch, and this was a big deal because the hotel and its food were quite elegant. We'd get dressed up in our fancy clothes to suit the occasion and the decor. It's funny the things you remember. I can't tell you what the Christmas menu was, but I do recall what my grandfather took home with him from the meal. I can still picture him filling up the pockets of his suit jacket with bread and rolls from the basket that was placed on the table. As a kid, I never questioned why he did that; in fact, I thought that that was what you were supposed to do. Grandpa would always explain his actions by saying, "Well, we shouldn't waste food, so we're taking this home." Now I think of him taking that bread (and the butter!) and I realize that having lived through the Depression, to him it all made perfect sense—and great memories.

My mom still lives in Florida, so on those alternate years when my husband and I are not in Pennsylvania, we're exchanging snow for sand as we spend Christmas at the beach. On my side of the family, we rent a big house, and whether it's 80 degrees or 30 degrees, we're there enjoying a different kind of Christmas environment. I know that some people may feel sorry for us Floridians not having the perfect Christmas card–esque experience, but I feel a tad guilty that a lot of people don't get to experience how awesome it is to be on the beach in late December instead of shoveling snow. Even as a kid, I thought I had gotten a pretty good deal by being born and raised in Florida. I never had to get all bundled up at Christmas. I loved going out and riding my new bicycle wearing shorts and a T-shirt.

Now, it did take my husband some time to get used to the Pennsylvania–Florida switch. We got married and moved to Florida, and around Christmastime, he said, "Where are the trees for the Christmas lights?" I explained to him that a palm tree is a tree, and they look very nice when illuminated. They do, and he's now adjusted, just so long as he gets his every-other-year dose of Pennsylvania Christmas.

I can now see that having two Christmases as a kid has continued, with some variation, into my adulthood, and, just as it was for me then, it's a very enjoyable combination.

Another ingredient of my combination Christmases was my late father. Among our must-watch Christmas movies each year are *White Christmas*, the sentimental story that brings tears to my eyes, and *National Lampoon's Christmas Vacation*, which also brings tears to my eyes but for a very different reason. Yes, I had a Clark W. Griswold in my life in the form of my father. He wanted every Christmas to be over-the-top with huge light displays, big gifts, all his kids around (me, my half brother, and my stepbrothers), but somehow, some way, things would go wrong in the most hilarious and frustrating ways for him.

He also frustrated us. The man could not just open a present! We laugh about it, but seriously, come on, Dad, just open it and stop trying to ruin the surprise! All his shaking and (almost-always-spot-on) guessing drained the surprise out of the process. It was no fun at all when he was right!

One Christmas he inadvertently got a taste of his own medicine. We were at Dad's house, and we were sitting with our packages in front of us, waiting to open them. It was obvious that one package in each of our piles was the same size and shape. My stepbrother opened his and inside was a portable TV, a little rectangular thing with an AM/FM receiver and a long whip of an antenna that never seemed to be able to bring in any stations. Well, it was a really nice gift, and the other three of us started to laugh when the next person in line chose his or her similar-looking package. My other stepbrother said, imitating Dad's usual routine, "Huh? I wonder what it is?" Dad did not look pleased.

To make things worse, we were interrupting the flow of the proceedings. Dad wanted us all to continue in a nice, orderly fashion while we opened our gifts one at a time, alternating from opener of gift to watcher of gift opener. Our shenanigans were upsetting the balance of Dad's Christmas universe.

For years after that, we would say to one another while opening presents, "I wonder what it is?" and my father's eyes would roll, remembering the year he got a great deal on those not-so-surprising TVs. We still share that story and still laugh and remain delighted by the memories of Clark, I mean Dad.

Having those merged-family Christmases was very nice, but there were a few years, especially when I was very young, when it was just Mom and me. She was a young mother, on a very limited budget, and I got used to hearing, "Things are tight this year, and Christmas isn't about presents, and please don't expect anything big, and I love you very much, but we just can't do that this year." I understood, and it was fine with me, and I was never aware that we didn't have everything we needed. Having a roof over my head, food to eat, and loving grandparents and parents was enough for me. And we had a lot of fun too. So when my mom would say that, I felt sad that she thought she had to lessen my expectations. That had to be hard for her, and yet, somehow, she always managed to put things under the tree for me.

One year after she'd married my stepdad—I must have been in third or fourth grade—I got something called a Sit 'n Spin. I'd seen commercials for it on television and I thought, "Gosh, wouldn't that be great!"

And it was!

If you don't remember it, the label on the box says it all. It was a plastic molded seat and pedestal and you would sit and spin on it, kind of like a home version of the playground piece. I spent hours on that thing, and I believe it was kind of a parent's best friend toy—I exhausted myself on it. Fortunately, I didn't get dizzy, just tired from all that exertion!

So, yes, money was tight in my childhood years, but I had so many blessings by being a branch on that complicated family tree. One of the greatest of those was the relationship I developed with my grandma Nell. She lived to 102, Grandpa Phil lived a good long life to 88, and we were close when I was a kid. I had a second kind of relationship with my grandma when I got older and we developed a true friendship. I adored her as a kid and admired her and appreciated her as an adult. As I aged, I was able to talk to her more about her life, the decisions she made as part of a married couple, that kind of thing.

We always went to church together for Christmas and the rest of the year. Years after Mom and I moved out and we all moved to Tallahassee, we would go to her house every Sunday to pick her up for services at Temple Baptist Church. Later on, when I was an adult, we'd still do this whenever I went home for a visit. Grandma Nell always wore a hat for services, and we always sat in the second row so that she could better hear the sermon and the songs. Regular church attendees knew that was Nell's spot, and we could tell that someone was new to the church if they settled in there. Grandma didn't mind at all; she loved getting to know guests and new church members.

That church figures into a lot of my Christmas memories of pageants and plays and choirs. Mom was a music teacher, a pianist and ukulele player, and a very fine vocalist. I play the piano and sing a little bit as well. As a young woman, I was involved in all the church programs, especially at Christmas, and I love, love, love Christmas music, reenactments of the Bible story of Jesus's birth, reading aloud from the Gospel of Luke 2, and choirs singing Christmas songs and hymns. My mom is still a very active participant in the music programs at church and its Christmas services.

I don't confine my enjoyment of Christmas music to November through December. I can be on a treadmill (I wish I still had that Sit 'n Spin!) at the gym in the middle of July and if a Christmas song comes up on my playlist, I'll never hit skip. It's more likely I'll pick up the pace since those songs energize me so much. I also love Christmas movies, and I've probably got at least ten Hallmark Channel ones stored in my DVR. I don't always have the time during the Christmas season to watch them when they're aired, but every now and then, when I'm feeling a little blue or under the weather, watching one is the medicine I need. They're the cure for whatever ails you.

Shannon's Christmas Playlist

"The First Noel"—by BeBe & CeCe Winans

"Gloria"—by Michael W. Smith

"A Strange Way to Save the World"—by 4Him

"Grown-Up Christmas List"—by Amy Grant

"All Is Well"—by Michael W. Smith and Carrie Underwood

"Don't Save It All for Christmas Day"—by Avalon
(with astronomically amazing lead vocals by my friend Jody McBrayer)

"Mary, Did You Know?"—by Michael English

The reason they work so well for me is they remind me of Christmas, and that means Jesus's and God's love for us and the joyous message of hope and redemption. Christmas is a birthday celebration, after all, and my birthday is wrapped up in the middle of the festivities. With Christmas, I love the idea that billions around the world are celebrating such a hopeful and happy event. I start early so I won't miss a drop of it. I don't want to be so busy I rush by the significance and the impact of Jesus's story and His presence here on earth. It offers encouragement for people of faith and those without it; it provides us with something to look forward to and the opportunity to serve others. People seem to be in a lighter mood, reaching out to friends and family more frequently, even to folks they don't know, and they offer help. That holiday spirit is such a beautiful thing.

One thing I think we often forget about the original Christmas is that while Jesus came to bring "peace on earth," He didn't arrive at a time of tranquil harmony and nostalgic cheer. His supernatural conception had cast his parents' lives into chaos, and the two young people were forced to struggle through His birth in a dirty barn, shared with animals. Later, the couple were refugees fleeing to Egypt, escaping a massacre by the skin of their teeth.

My reasoning for bringing up these sad events is not to cast a pall over the holiday but to remind us that no matter how difficult times seem, we can still feel the thrill that Mary, Joseph, and the shepherds must have *known* as they realized that God had literally been born in the midst of this turbulence.

This is why we celebrate Christmas with feasting and festivities. I've found it brings me great joy even when times are tough.

Christmas reminds me how blessed I am. I feel the same way I did as a child—I have a roof over my head, food, medical care, basics that not every human being has. People are struggling around the world and in our own communities. Through our church, my family participates in various charitable outreach programs, mainly providing food or gifts for people who find themselves in need. Many years ago, we did one that was Christmas-related. Church members purchased gifts and wrapped them. We drove around town to deliver the presents to families in need so that the families could give them to the kids either from Santa Claus or from them. At one house, the mom was really sweet and invited us in. Her kids ran up to greet us. One said, "Come, look at our Christmas tree!" We followed her into the living room, and taped to a wall was a photograph of a Christmas tree that they'd trimmed from a magazine.

That immediately put things into perspective for me. I knew that I had not a single thing to complain about. These people were joyful in what they had. We thought we were going there to bless them, but it was the other way around. I knew that I should always be grateful, and that Christmas, those kids brought that lesson home to me in the most vivid way possible. Along with being thankful, we can all get creative in the midst of difficult circumstances.

Now, I'm in no way comparing having to work on Christmas to the situation that family was in, but this is a funny little Christmas story from a few years ago when I was away from family on Christmas Day and missing everyone. I was on and off air frequently throughout the day, doing quick news updates on the half hour. I decided that for fun, I'd switch outfits for every appearance. It took my mom, who watches everything I do, a few hours to figure it out. A few people on social media responded after that as well.

I'm often working around Christmas, and in 2019, I took my then assistant Anna and one of FOX's amazing hair and makeup artists, Melyssa, with me to see the Rockettes. I'm a sucker for the Rockettes and they'd never been. We played hooky from work, sat in our seats, and started sharing this amazing treat—a bucket of chocolate chip cookies you can actually buy at Radio City Music Hall. A child seated in front of us was a bit squirmy, and when he looked back and spotted us— three grown women—munching away, his face lit up! We asked his mom if it was okay if we shared our snack with them. She said, "Sure!" It's that kind of small gesture, sharing something simple with a stranger, that really makes Christmas Christmas. I love New York during the holidays, and DC is wonderful, but what I'm really looking forward to is the next time we can all be at Aunt Dink's house to celebrate. It wasn't the punch that I missed in 2020, but being together with all our loved ones gathered in one spot, enjoying one another's company, all of us grateful, all of us looking around the room to see who's playing Santa this year. But, you know, we can all be givers, and not just at Christmas, but all year.

Now, whether you want to wear Aunt Dink's Santa suit is another matter. Merry Christmas!

Shannon Bream currently serves as the anchor of *FOX News @ Night with Shannon Bream* (weekdays 12–1 a.m. ET).

Lauren Green

*Lauren Green reflects on how her understanding of
Christmas has evolved with her development in faith.*

For me, my memories of Christmas spanning childhood to adulthood represent, in some measure, the evolution of my Christian faith. What began as
a childhood fantasy of Santa Claus, reindeer, toys, and all the rest of the
secular traditions we share in our culture, has, over time, taken on the full theological weight of the reality of Jesus Christ being born. One way to illustrate this
is that as a child I sang Christmas carols and hymns. I knew the words. As I got
older I understood the meaning of the words. I now understand and appreciate

Lauren Green loves the way Christmas hymns recall
the true meaning of Christmas.

these wonderful theological truths in the nugget and the form of a familiar tune. They are just so powerful.

Christmas hymns are important for three reasons. First, they remind us of the power of the Gospel. Second, God gave us the skill and the command to sing, and He can be glorified even in good secular music. And finally, they remind us of our complete reliance on the grace of God.

One of the hymns I just love is "Hark! The Herald Angels Sing." The carol describes a scene that Luke relates in chapter 2, verse 14. Two of the founding ministers of Methodism, George Whitefield and Charles Wesley, contributed to the lyrics, which are set to the music of Felix Mendelssohn, the great German composer famous for the oratorios *St. Paul* and *Elijah*. The song begins with "Hark! the herald angels sing, 'Glory to the newborn king. Peace on earth and mercy mild, God and sinners reconciled.' " That last statement, "God and sinners reconciled," reflects what Jesus was born to do and heralded for all mankind. Humanity can now be reconciled with God, because God chose to send His son to us as a gift, creating a chance for our relationship with Him to be reconciled. We sin but we can be redeemed through God's grace. That is what makes Christianity what it is. Later lyrics say, "Veiled in flesh the Godhead see. Hail the incarnate deity." That tells us that God has come in the flesh. He is an incarnate deity. He is, as the Gospel writer John says, "The Word made flesh." Those few verses are the summation of, the foundational beliefs that underpin, our faith.

Another example that so many people love is "Joy to the world! the Lord is come; let earth receive her king. Let every heart prepare Him room and heaven and nature sing . . . Joy to the world! the savior reigns . . . No more let sin and sorrow grow . . . He rules the world with truth and grace and makes the nations prove the glories of His righteousness and wonders of His love." That is, again, a very succinct presentation of the Gospels, in this case in four verses.

I didn't know that as a child, and now I can't even think of some of these verses and these carols without weeping because of their power and their beauty.

"O come, all ye faithful, joyful and triumphant. O come ye, o come ye to Bethlehem. Come and behold Him, born the king of angels." Oh my goodness, how powerful that is!

One of the reasons why I host a caroling party every year is so that people can join together to sing those hymns again. And we sing other songs as well—"White Christmas," "Silver Bells," "The Christmas Song."

Besides the power of these songs to proclaim the Gospel, we sing because we are commanded to make music by God. And every heart, really, when it sings, is ultimately singing to God. We might be singing, "Chestnuts roasting on an open fire," but the warmth and comfort that we're seeking through that song is really our heart crying out to God to comfort us. And so, more than two hundred times in the book of Psalms, we are commanded to sing to God. That's the second-most commanded thing in the book of Psalms. That's how important music is to God, to us all, and why it is to me.

Now, when God says that to us, what is He telling us? It means that there's something about singing that moves us, that lifts us up. It's more than icing on the cake. When you are enjoying anything, witnessing something beautiful, you have to sing about it, because singing invites others to join in with you. Singing *hymns* together transforms and inspires us; it makes us aware of the true meaning of life. Singing Christmas carols together is the glorification of the God we worship through song.

In Genesis we learn about God creating the world through His voice: "And God said, let there be light." C. S. Lewis, the great theologian, wrote of God creating the world through singing, not just a speaking voice, but one raised up in song, through the implement of music. Psalm 19 talks about the heavens declaring the glory of God, and the words will proclaim His majesty. Day after day, they pour forth speech and song. There is something in our nature that constantly pours out our knowledge of God and our special role in His plan.

I'm partial to that perspective because music has meant so much to me throughout my life. I graduated from the University of Minnesota with a bachelor's degree in piano performance. I do enjoy singing as well. I'm not a "singer" singer—I wouldn't be able to join a professional choir or dare sing a solo in public—but I do love to sing, especially after a couple of glasses of wine consumed during my caroling party!

On that night of caroling, we sing with piano accompaniment, but I also love when carols are sung with a backing orchestra and in full four-part harmony. I'll tell you, there is just something so incredibly moving about that, all those human voices joined together to sing God's praises. One of my favorite, favorite pieces, of course, is Handel's *Messiah*. It's sung mostly at Christmas, although it's not really a Christmas-only oratorio. It is also an Easter and the victory of Resurrection piece. After all, Easter is the cornerstone of the faith. The *Messiah* relates to the entire biblical narrative of redemption, of the Messiah's birth, death, redemption, salvation. You could say, and I have written as much in my book *Lighthouse Faith*, that Handel's *Messiah* is a Cliffs Notes version of the Holy Scriptures—it's all there and I so enjoy it.

I used to work as an usher at Orchestra Hall in Minneapolis, the main home of the Minnesota Orchestra. Each December they would do a series of about five or six performances of Handel's *Messiah*. It was a big deal and a lot of people wanted to attend. I was fortunate to work pretty much all of those nights and was able to hear it and the famous "Hallelujah Chorus." One performance was always at the Cathedral of Saint Paul in Saint Paul, Minnesota. To hear it in a cathedral, with statues of the four authors of the Gospels in the building's corners, with this magnificent dome supported by those flying buttresses, was a revelation! That dome reverberated with the music and the voices of the triumphant "Hallelujah Chorus," and the words and music were more than divinely inspired. My knees buckled to hear it, and to experience those sounds in the space that is specially devoted to God was very, very special.

The *Messiah* is in three parts. The first is the one that relates to Christmas most directly—His birth. The second relates to the story of the suffering servant and what He came to do, and that part is based primarily on the prophesies of Isaiah in the Old Testament. It's at the end of that section that the "Hallelujah Chorus" is sung. This suffering servant has been crucified, but now He's risen, and, hallelujah! The God omnipotent reigns. That is so powerful! The final part is really one long song of victory, "Worthy is the lamb that was slain and hath redeemed us to God." It ends, as does our prayers, with "Amen." That oratorio, just like some carols, encapsulates the grand narrative of our entire existence.

That's one of the reasons why I cringe every time I hear the "Hallelujah Chorus" being used in commercials. The same with "Christmas Bells," to which the words are "Ring, Christmas Bells, sound far and near, the birthday of Jesus is here. Herald the News, to old and young, tell it to all in every tongue." It breaks my heart to hear those songs being used to hawk products.

But that doesn't mean I can't appreciate the way the truth can shine through even secular Christmas traditions. As a child, I knew about and believed in the traditional figure in the red suit who flew through the sky to deliver gifts all around the world. When I'm asked when I stopped believing in Santa Claus, I reply, "I never really stopped believing in Santa Claus." I still believe in Santa Claus because I know that he is the embodiment of the spirit of giving that was demonstrated by the real-life person known as St. Nicholas. (I was married in St. Nicholas Greek Orthodox Shrine Church, by the way.) He performed many works of charity to help relieve the burden of poverty he saw in his community. So, in Santa giving gifts, in us giving them to one another, we are honoring that man, the original Santa Claus, and his mission.

This is why I often enjoy the other, less spiritual or religious elements of Christmas. I love them and have created some traditions for my own family. I do what I refer to as the Community Gift and the Calico Christmas Gift. I began these many years ago, and the first one involves buying and wrapping in identical paper the same gift. Sometimes I put it in a big, personalized bag that I ordered related to the year or something like that. One year, I gave everyone in the family red socks—you'd be surprised how difficult it is to find red socks that span the age range from children to adults! I've done scarves—a red-and-white striped one—a book, like James K. A. Smith's *On the Road with St. Augustine*, to name a few. We open those first, but not before I speak with my assembled family to tell them that Jesus is really the gift of Christmas. We give these gifts to one another because we're so grateful for what we've already been given in the death and Resurrection of Jesus Christ, whose birthday we're now celebrating.

The second gift, the Calico Gift, is one larger thing, something very nice, that has to be shared. One person wins the drawing for it. Since it's something to be shared, more than one person will be enjoying it. I've put a television set and various DVDs in the Calico Gift box; it has been a set of bowls along with cake or other food mixes, that kind of thing. Why is it a Calico Gift? you might be wondering. I put the gift, no matter its size, into a large box. I then wrap it by using the ends of all the other wrapping paper rolls I've used to that point in that year's wrapping or leftovers from previous years. That patchwork of swatches and cellophane tape Band-Aids looks terrible, but that's the point. I tell the family, "You know, sometimes the gift that looks the worst to us turns out to be the best!" I relate that to Christ. In the Bible, the Prophet Isaiah speaks of Jesus as not having an appearance that would draw you to Him. On the outside, Jesus was unremarkable, a man not so different from any other. But there He was, the Son of God, God made into flesh. The man, the gift from God, that you never would have thought of as physically beautiful, turned out to be the very essence of our being. That was my inspiration for the Calico Gift.

I believe that if I can make those two speeches before presenting those two gifts, then I've done my part to unite the secular and the sacred. I do that for my family knowing that a lot of young people don't want to be at church, they don't want someone preaching at them about what faith is. They want to be "spiritual but not religious." I get that. I was like that too. It usually takes life getting really hard and stressful for you to start searching for something larger than yourself. When you went to college, did you complete all your studies dutifully and well but still your career isn't shaping up how you'd imagined it might? You did the same with relationships, put in the effort, but still . . . That's when people start looking at the bigger picture; they start thinking more about their life's meaning. Hopefully my words and my music can penetrate those hardened exteriors so that, at some point, those not fully engaged or engaged at all will come to a deeper faith.

I understand that disconnect among faith, belief, spirit, and religion because that's what I lived. I grew up in a household where we didn't go to church on Christmas Eve or Christmas Day. That was just not something we did. That wasn't something that any of the members of the Black church, the African-American Methodist Episcopal church we attended, did. That wasn't a part of the tradition. It wasn't that I didn't know or appreciate the story of Christ's birth, but, as I say, there was that disconnect between knowing about the Three Wise Men, the Star of Bethlehem, and the rest of the biblical Christmas story and actually attending services that day. I never really understood why that was so, and as an adult, I've attended many, many Christmas Eve services and look forward to them every year.

And yet, despite that gap in church attendance, when I was growing up, my community was saturated in Christmas traditions. I never had to question my faith because everyone at my school believed the same thing. We always referred to our time off for Christian holidays as Christmas break, and in the spring it was Easter break. It wasn't the holiday break or the spring break.

I remember when I was six years old and we had a Christmas concert at our school. I was in the first grade. Our class was assigned to sing "Away in a Manger." I was one of three girls who actually sang the third verse without the rest of the class joining in. This was at a public school. No one challenged the idea of singing Christmas songs there; that was what everyone was doing. And in the larger community, stores would place Nativity scenes in their windows, and Stars of Bethlehem were hung more abundantly than stockings.

I love that people want to teach their children to give and have this philanthropic view of what Christmas brings to the heart, this giving spirit. But one of the problems is, if you don't connect it to the Gospel, it becomes about you.

And that brings me to my final reason for why Christmas hymns are so important. They remind us of our place in the great tapestry of God's design, which gives us the clarity to be humble and confident in God's love. Christmas is about more than just us. If Christmas is just about you showing how wonderful you are because of what you're *giving* to people, you contribute and receive a short-lived kind of benefit, *but* you don't understand the Gospel and why Christ was born. And this is my problem with the secular world saying you should just be a loving person and that's it. Well, that's fine, to be a loving person, but why are you a loving person? Are you loving to get love in return? Are you loving to feel good about yourself? Are you loving *just* to show God that He owes you? Because then it's all about you. What is the meaning of life? What is the purpose of life? And the purpose of life . . . I'm going to go into a theological point of view here . . . is to glorify God. We are here. We are born to worship, but we have a choice of what to worship. But if we are worshipping anything other than God, then that thing is going to disappoint us.

I love giving, and my church does a lot of ministries to reach out to the homeless, to raise funds for toys or gifts and presents for people who won't have enough, that I give through. And there are plenty of opportunities to give even in your circle. There are plenty of people who are right next to you, especially in a place like Manhattan, where you see homeless people on the streets all the time and give to them. You can give them money on the street or you can point them toward things like the Bowery Mission, which is directed toward helping people on a longer-term basis.

I was listening to a friend of mine, who is really one of my spiritual mentors, and she's in her late eighties, but she's so vibrant and she is such a wonderful woman of faith. And she was talking about the philanthropic opportunities that

God presents us with. There are opportunities all the way around, but sometimes we forget that the people who need us might be our neighbors next to us.

Yes, we need to give to the poor. But then, just as Jesus talks about the poor in spirit, there are people who need our help but don't need financial assistance. They need a shoulder to cry on. They need a friend who will listen to their pains and their sorrows. Sometimes we think that if somebody has all the money in the world and all the resources, they don't hurt or need a listening ear. But there is such a thing as the poor in spirit. There are so many aspects and facets of this world that take us away from God, that detract from our really seeking God.

So if Christmas is God coming in the flesh, God breaking through our world and coming in the flesh to heal us, to heal this world, then we can bring heaven to earth by extending that love and kindness to our fellow human beings. That's when heaven and nature can sing. That's when we can all bring joy to some part of our world.

To one degree or another, everyone wants the world to change, but it's like, "Are you willing to change yourself? How willing are you to change yourself?" The Catholic writer G. K. Chesterton talked about this. In one famous moment, Chesterton wrote a response to an article in the London *Daily News* that posed the question: "What is wrong with the world?" Chesterton chimed in with the pithy answer: "I am." He continued, "Until a man can give that answer his idealism is only a hobby." His meaning was that until we recognize the flaw in ourselves, we can never make true and effective change in the world. Recognizing that we are the problem should spur us to acknowledge that we have to be more than free; we have to fulfill our duties to each other.

It is so powerful, so transformative, when we can examine ourselves instead of pointing a finger of blame. "What's wrong with the world? Me." It's my pride, my unforgiveness, my self-righteousness, my anger, my jealousy . . . the list is endless, really. What happens to me, to my community, to my family and friends when I have a mean-spirited evil inside me that I have never checked, and I allow it to go unchecked on and on? And what if I blame everybody else for my problems? What does that say? What am I saying?

Instead, our thoughts could be, "I am the problem. I am a sinner and I have not recognized it. But now I recognize it. I am a sinner saved by grace," and that's why those Christmas carols mean so much. "Veiled in flesh, the Godhead see, hail the incarnate deity. Peace with men meant to dwell, Jesus our Immanuel." God is with us.

You understand the power of the Gospel only when you understand the depth of your own sin. I cannot save myself, and I have tried. We've all tried. Salvation by works is the default mode of every human heart. But it's short-lived. In the end if we're honest we'll say, "I cannot save myself. I need a savior, and I'm willing to admit it. And the only way I can be saved is just to say I'm powerless to really save myself to get right with God."

God gave us the gift of His son to show us the way toward salvation. That's why we celebrate Christmas, that's why we go home to be with family, that's why we go to God's house to celebrate with Him. And there, in our homes and in our churches, we lift up our voices in song to Him who is our Savior, our Redeemer.

Lauren Green currently serves as FOX News Channel's chief religion correspondent based in the New York bureau.

Geraldo Rivera

For Geraldo, finding just the right balance between his Catholic and Jewish heritage was a struggle during childhood Decembers, but the Rivera family eventually decided on a "Chrismukkah" compromise.

When I think of Christmas and my family, I can't help but think of it as a love story. The Bible story, of course, involves Jesus and his parents, Joseph and Mary. What a love story that is, but my parents' union and how my memories of Christmas are tied up in their love and marriage are what often come to my mind.

My dad, Cruz Rivera, was one of seventeen children from the Rivera family of Bayamón, Puerto Rico. His family members worked in the sugarcane fields of the island. In 1940, he came to the United States, literally on the United

Geraldo, wife Erica, sister Sharon, daughter Sol, and mother Lil.

Fruit Company banana boat that stopped once a week in San Juan and then came to New York Harbor. He got a job in the kitchen of Childs restaurant, which at the time was located at Forty-Second Street and Sixth Avenue in New York. My dad was bilingual and also the first in his huge family to graduate high school. Because he could speak both English and Spanish, along with his other jobs he would translate management's requests to the mostly Puerto Rican kitchen staff. My dad was dashing, with wavy black hair and a little mustache. You could tell him from a mile away. Desi Arnaz, from *I Love Lucy*, a fellow Spanish-speaking immigrant, was his role model and his hero. My dad was also religious and a lay deacon in the Catholic Church, which meant he could perform some ministerial functions.

My mom, Lily Friedman, one of eight children from Newark, New Jersey, was as stereotypical as my dad in her own way. She was from a conservative religious Jewish family who practiced their faith with real devotion.

So my mom and dad came from two wildly different worlds. As a young woman my mom was a waitress in Childs restaurant; my dad was in charge of the pot washers. They met and fell in love. Initially, my dad agreed to change his faith and become, nominally, Jewish. Even though he was a very religious Catholic, he was so in love with my mother that he agreed with her parents to waive his Catholicism and convert, although I don't believe he went through any formal theological process. He portrayed himself as Jewish, at least in his early married years.

That was okay when it was just my sister Irene and me. Initially, when we kids were born, we lived first on the Lower East Side and then in Williamsburg, Brooklyn. Ultimately, we were five kids, but at that time it was just the two of us. And we were basically raised as Jewish kids. Both of those places had fairly substantial populations of Jews living there. I remember going to temple with my grandfather, who had a very stern and scary demeanor. He was kind of fierce, at least that's the way it seemed to me then, and going to the temple in Williamsburg was a serious endeavor.

In time, my dad went from the restaurant to driving a taxi. He worked several jobs to support us all. He reminded me of the character in *In Living Color* who asked, "How many jobs you got?" My dad worked really, really hard. He was an army veteran from World War II, a former staff sergeant. Even though the military was segregated in those days, again because of his fluency in English and Spanish, his job was often to act as liaison with the Puerto Rican troops.

At a certain point around the very early 1950s (I was born in 1943), my dad decided that he'd take advantage of the GI Bill's benefits that were available. At the time, in recognition of their service, veterans could get a ten-thousand-dollar mortgage almost fully funded by the government. So Dad decided to move us when we were in grade school to West Babylon, Long Island. He also had gotten a job at the Republic Aviation Corporation, working at that defense plant's kitchen. Moving out of the city was a big step up.

On Long Island, away from the influence of my mother's parents, Mom and Dad engaged in a constant struggle between my father's Catholicism and my mother's Judaism. By this time, more members of my father's huge family were moving to the United States, and I'm sure they exerted some influence on him, wondering how he could have given up his faith and exchanged it for another. My mother knew that my father had made a deal with her parents, and with her, to adopt Judaism and to raise us kids as Jews.

So Christmas crystallized the whole epic ethnic struggle between these very stereotypical people, my Jewish mom and my Puerto Rican dad. As I remember, my mom prevailed in the early years and we did not recognize Christmas, although in school it was very difficult for us because, as I recall, we were the first Jewish family in West Babylon, a community of working-class Irish and Italian families. And at the time Wyandanch, the Black community, was part of our school system. But there were no Jews at all, only us. I remember taking Jewish holidays off and feeling that we were the oddballs. "What's wrong with us? Why are we taking off? It's embarrassing," and so forth.

Also, most of my friends were Catholic. I remember we hung out with Vinnie and Frank Simone, who were my best friends. They were very Catholic and they lived down the block. Anyway, my point of view developed into this: It's hard to be Jewish. I didn't want to be Jewish. I drifted away from Judaism almost as soon as we got to Long Island and resented deeply the fact that we did not have a Christmas tree. So the Christmas tree became the focal point of the entire epic struggle between the Jewish half and the Puerto Rican half of my family.

We constantly lobbied my mom. We implored my dad. "Why don't we have Christmas? Why can't we have a Christmas tree? We want Christmas. Everyone else has one!" We didn't believe in Santa Claus, obviously. We were too old for that. I was just about to enter my teens. My mother said, "Not only are we not having a Christmas tree, Geraldo, but you're going to be bar mitzvahed."

So I had to study for and be instructed in everything I needed for my bar mitzvah. At the service, which was held at the volunteer fire department hall in North Lindenhurst, the town next to West Babylon, on the other side of the tracks, the number of Catholic Puerto Ricans clearly outnumbered by a long shot the number of Jews. Not only was my mother's family smaller than my father's, but they would have had to travel a long way to attend. I can still recall that when it came time for a solemn reading of a portion of the Torah, all my Puerto Rican family members took off their yarmulkes to place them over their hearts. That's not appropriate at a Jewish ceremony, but they were trying to be respectful.

When you are bar mitzvahed it's like you are recognized as a man, an adult. Shortly after my bar mitzvah, my sister Irene and I said to my mom—my sister Irene had dumped Judaism by that time and become a devout Catholic—we said, "Mom, we're having a Christmas tree no matter what." My mom did not agree. It was a tearful scene. She went into her room, and we conspired to get a Christmas tree. As a consolation to my mother, we called it a Hanukkah bush, and we called the holiday Chrismukkah. So I remember very clearly our first Christmas tree and calling it the Hanukkah bush, and my mom's initial resentment and resistance. Gradually, she relented a bit and agreed with us about having a tree and being multicultural about it. And we always sang, I remember, along with "Jingle Bells" and "White Christmas" and all that, we always would sing the hymn "Rock of Ages" to give my mother some comfort—not that that's a particularly Jewish song, but just a non-Catholic song.

So we had the Hanukkah bush, we celebrated Chrismukkah, and I don't know when I stopped taking Jewish holidays off from work, but I entered the Catholic phase of my life. I would come and go. I was Catholic for a couple of years, and then there was a terrorist incident in Israel, the Ma'alot Massacre, they called it. And I was reminded that no matter what we celebrated, I was still Jewish.

To honor that side of my family, I got a Star of David tattoo on my left hand. I can't say it was entirely my dad's influence, but when I was old enough to date and to consider marriage and family, I always decided that religion—the religion of the family, the children—would follow the mother. I just decided that. Like in the Jewish religion, they say the mother is dominant. In the Catholic religion, it's the exact opposite. It's the father who determines the religion. But I raised my children as whatever their mother was. So I had a Jewish son. Then I had a Catholic son. Then I had two Episcopalian daughters. Then I had a Jewish daughter. So that accounts for my five children. And now we celebrate both Hanukkah and Christmas, but separately. There's no more Hanukkah bush. There's no Christmas tree at all now with Erica, my Jewish wife. But we do celebrate Christmas and we celebrate Hanukkah as well. Erica likes lighting the candles, and that's our Christmas now. It's Christmas with a menorah.

I'm not exaggerating at all when I say that we were the only Jewish family in our neighborhood in West Babylon. That was tough to deal with. We were also the only Puerto Rican family. So, in my mind, it was a toss-up between whether it was harder to be a Jew or a Puerto Rican. I'm glad that now I'm comfortable being both, but it wasn't always like that. I even remember that, because of peer pressure, I went to confession in the Catholic church with my buddies Vinnie and Frank. I wanted to do what everyone else was doing. I was trying so hard to fit in. Fortunately for me, each Christmas that went on, my mom relaxed a bit, and her objections to the tree and our celebrating a non-Jewish holiday weren't as big of a deal to her.

I don't mean to imply that the holidays were fraught with tension and bad feelings. They weren't. My parents were both determined to provide us with a good life. It's funny to think about how passionate my dad was about assimilating. He wanted us to be Americans first and Puerto Ricans and Jews second. He was a pragmatically conservative Republican—he even wanted me to vote for Richard Nixon over John F. Kennedy, a Catholic. My dad was all about having an "American" Christmas, listening to Bing Crosby records and watching Jimmy Stewart in *It's a Wonderful Life*. That's what he wanted for us—a wonderful life. Eventually other members of his family came to the mainland, and I have more than a hundred first cousins here in the US in my generation.

It can't get any more American than having a toy train circling the tree. I remember that for years the other kids would come back to school after the Christmas break telling us what they got. I didn't get to do that for quite a while, but when I did, nothing made me happier than talking about the Lionel train I finally got. I loved the design of trains, and every year for a number of years, I had one of those steel-and-iron Lionel toy trains on the top of my list. My dad never earned much—I think he likely never made more than ten thousand dollars a year—so it took a long time before he and my mom were able to make that wish come true. I ran the hell out of that train, setting up tracks that took it on tours of the living room, around the tree, under the couch. For a few years after getting that first set, I'd always get a couple more cars. I think I was as excited as anyone when I was able to buy a set for my oldest grandson, Jace. What a joy that was.

Not all my memories of Christmas bring up images of smiling faces and expressions of pleasure. For many years, along with my brother, Craig, who works with me as my producer, I spent Christmas in war zones. More than once we were in Baghdad, Iraq, or at Bagram Airfield outside Kabul, Afghanistan. We were there to cover Operation Iraqi Freedom and Operation Enduring Freedom that the US undertook as part of the global war on terrorism. I remember once when Craig complained to our boss that our overseas assignments in late November and December were taking us away from our families during the holidays, and he said, "Your kids won't remember." I don't know how true that is, but I remember a lot of times when we weren't spending time with family from 2001 to 2012. The troops, of course, had it far worse than we did, but we spent a lot of time in forward operating bases, consuming packaged meals ready to eat (MREs). There was one time when we were in Jalal-Abad at Thanksgiving. Craig and I, along with a number of other correspondents and crews, were staying at the Jalalabad Hotel. We chipped in to buy a turkey. What we received was a scrawny chicken. Over the years we ate our share of MREs with cranberry sauce. A couple of times we did get a real turkey meal. One of those times was when Senators Hillary Clinton and Jack Reed were out there.

My family certainly felt my absence over the years, but they understood the nature of my work. I usually brought back gifts that local artisans had crafted from whatever area I was in. I don't think that anyone was waiting with bated breath for those to show up under the tree, but I thought they were a fine way to remember those people and those places.

I also loved traveling to Puerto Rico to visit family there. A few times, a family reunion coincided with a Christmas trip to the island. Being back there among my dad's siblings and my tribe of cousins, I came to understand the great Puerto Rican ethnic story. From black to white, their skin tones were a reflection of Puerto Rican history. Among the mix we even had a few redheads. My grandma Tomasa was very significantly Taino, native in appearance with high cheekbones, very Indian in the old sense of that word. It's wonderful to think that my grandparents produced seventeen children, and then they produced their own kids, and in quite a variety of shapes, sizes, and colors.

If you haven't had a whole roasted pig or pasteles wrapped in banana leaves—they're a kind of pastry with a hummus-like filling—then you haven't experienced all the splendors of Christmas. In fact, my mouth is watering right now thinking of delicious treats. For almost fifteen years, we owned a small island three miles off the Puerto Rican coast, immodestly called Cayo Geraldo. I loved being able to re-create there the Christmas celebrations that my grandparents used to host. We had local entertainers come in to play salsa music. Erica understood that these celebrations were as much a celebration of my family and its history as they were of Jesus's birth. Besides, how can you not enjoy a family get-together that combines rum, tequila, abundant sunshine, and a lot of dancing?

Our Christmases may not bring up visions of a typical Christmas-card scene, but they do reflect who we are and our family's history. Those days are filled with a lot of expressions of love, and that's really what the spirit of the season is all about.

Geraldo Rivera currently serves as a roaming correspondent at large for FOX News Channel.

Rachel Campos-Duffy
and Sean Duffy

*Now it's our turn to reflect on the joys of melding varying
family traditions while always remembering that Christmas
is truly about God's greatest gift: His son.*

Rachel: Catholic traditions formed my earliest memories of Christmas and deeply shaped my family's practices for the holiday. In my childhood home, Christmas was truly a religious holiday, and we took very seriously the liturgical season of Advent. Those four weeks of preparation leading up to Christmas were a time when many parts of our faith really came into focus as we prepared for the birth of our Savior. Like many families, we had an Advent wreath and candles. Now that we are parents ourselves, we are very intentional

The Duffy family starts Christmas early, celebrating the season of Advent.

about Advent rituals since it is the best way to remind our children of the religious meaning of Christmas. Every evening during Advent, our kids really love turning off all the lights in the house and watching the flickering candles of our Advent wreath. Our nightly prayers involve not just lighting the candle and praying but also singing "O Come, O Come, Emmanuel."

Since none of us is a great singer, Sean has his favorite version, by Enya, ready on iTunes for our nightly family ritual. I also take time at the start of Advent to set our family altar for the Advent season with the kids, placing a statue of St. Nicholas and three boxes representing the gifts that the Magi bring the baby Jesus. I also place a basket with a baby Jesus doll and a jar of hay next to it. Throughout the season, we encourage our children to perform good deeds, and with each good deed, they place a piece of hay under the baby Jesus. The goal is to do so many good deeds that you prepare a soft bed for the baby Jesus in time for Christmas. But of course, with each good deed, we also prepare our hearts.

In Hispanic culture, the Nativity scene plays a central and important role in decorating one's home for Christmas. When I was growing up, my mother didn't just put up the normal manger scene with the Holy Family and the Three Kings. She built the whole town of Bethlehem for us, complete with a river, mountains, the cave where the angels greeted the shepherds, and even Herod's castle. As a military family, we traveled extensively, and wherever we went in the world—Europe, Latin America, and the Middle East—my mom would make a point of purchasing something for our family's Nativity scene. As a result, our Nativity scene had an international flavor and it didn't necessarily stick to the time period. On the sawdust path that led to the manger, you might find a pilgrim, an African drummer, or even Tom from *Tom and Jerry*. My mom would explain that Jesus was for all people and for all ages.

It was so exciting as a child to help my mom and dad set up the Nativity scene. There were rocks, moss, twinkling lights, and so many beautiful angels. We learned so much about the story of Christmas as we unwrapped the figurines and many fragile components of this little work of art.

Soon after I started having children, my mom gifted me the entire Nativity scene. Every year she would ask me if I was going to set it up. For some reason, I could never bring myself to do it, partly out of fear that I could not do it or complete the process and partly out of feeling too exhausted to do such a big project around the holidays. I kept wondering how my own mother could have put it up (and taken it down!) all those years when we were growing up, especially since we were a military family who moved every three to four years.

For twenty years, I neglected the most important and formative of all her childhood family traditions. I felt guilty for not carrying it on, and each year that passed I promised myself that next year, when I wasn't pregnant, or nursing, or quite as tired, I would finally do it. But alas, it never happened, until this past year when COVID hit.

One of the silver linings of the COVID-19 pandemic was that my parents, who live in Arizona and were lonely, missing their grandkids, and sick and tired of the lockdowns, decided to spend a month with us for Christmas! Immediately, my mom determined that this would finally be the year she taught me and the kids how to set up the elaborate family Nativity scene. It's hard for me to describe the joy I experienced seeing my childhood memories unwrapped after so many years. Even more precious was seeing my mom and dad with my own kids, patiently and lovingly re-creating this beautiful treasure.

When I was growing up, our family Nativity was so beautiful that friends and family (sometimes our class at school!) would come to our home to see it. It was unusual for a private home to have such a large Christmas display. Normally, you could see something like that only in a church. In Spain, where I lived for five years in elementary school, many churches had gorgeous Nativity scenes, and some were so elaborate and special that people would travel beyond their local parish to view them.

There was something special about those Nativity scenes in Zaragoza and throughout Spain, set inside or outside churches and cathedrals that dated back centuries. I was deeply influenced by the beauty, art, and architecture of European cathedrals. The statues, the candles, and the incense reminded me that I am part of something so ancient and beautiful. As a kid, I loved going to midnight mass on Christmas Eve; I always felt like I was being transported back in time. The soft light and the shadows in the church seemed fitting; it was so easy to imagine Jesus, Joseph, and Mary inside that dimly lit stable, the farm animals standing near. It truly brought that first Christmas to life.

A few years back, our daughter Paloma was told she was going to be part of the St. Anne Catholic School Nativity play. Every day she would tell me how much she wanted to be selected to be the Virgin Mary in the play. That year, we took a family trip to New York City at Christmastime. On the walk from Rockefeller Center, where we viewed the giant Christmas tree, to St. Patrick's Cathedral, where we would be attending mass, Paloma reminded me that her teacher would be announcing the roles for the school Nativity play the following week. Once again, she expressed her desire to be Mary. While inside the beautiful St. Patrick's Cathedral, I kneeled with her in front of a statue of Mary and we lit a candle together. I told her to pray and ask Our Lady to let her be Mary in the Christmas play. "Pray and it might happen," I reassured her.

Well, the next week, when she wasn't chosen to be Mary, I felt terrible. I wondered what damage I might have done to her faith. To my great relief, Paloma took it well and embraced her role as a sheep. A few days later, after one of her play rehearsals, she burst out of the school doors and toward my car with immeasurable excitement. As she got into the car, a look of glee I will never forget spread across her face.

"Mom! Mom!" she said.

"What is it?"

"The most amazing thing happened!"

"What?"

"Mary decided she wants to be a donkey!"

"Come again?" I asked, totally confused.

"Mom! Mary decided she wanted to be a donkey, so now I get to be Mary!"

It was a Christmas miracle I will never forget!

I know that you love that Paloma story too, Sean, but why don't you tell us more about what it was like to celebrate Christmas in northern Wisconsin.

Sean: I was raised Catholic too, but a lot of my earliest and fondest memories of Christmas aren't quite as peaceful and reverent as yours are of going to midnight mass. I'm the tenth of eleven children, which means we had a whole lot of people at our house at Christmas. It was fun, it was raucous, and it was pure chaos at times! There is a twenty-year age gap from youngest to oldest, and believe it or not, my mom had eight of us in the first ten years. Then she took a break and had the last three of us during that second decade. In other words, I was one of the babies, which is why so many of my memories of Christmas have to do with older siblings coming back from college or returning with their spouses and kids. It also means that as a kid, I got exposed to some "bigger kid" things.

Duffy family Christmas gatherings involved playing board games, swapping stories, telling a few off-color jokes, and, of course, being from Wisconsin, some (or a lot) of beer consumption. I also remember the noise level with everyone seemingly talking and laughing all at once.

To be sure, it never devolved into a wild college frat-house party or anything like that; it was just that I was surrounded by a lot of adults and college kids and everyone was in happy spirits.

As a family, we celebrated a very traditional all American kind of Christmas. Even if we didn't have extended family over, our house was always full of people. Sometimes, my older siblings led me into temptation. Specifically, that meant one or more of them leading me down into the basement, where we kept a chest freezer. As Christmas approached, we were admonished to stay out of that freezer. That was because at just about the same time as Rachel was beginning her family's Advent observances, we were observing a greater-than-normal amount of activity in the kitchen. My mother went into baking overdrive, knowing how many cookies she was going to have to bake for eleven kids, their friends, and any guests that dropped by. First, I have to say that my mom bakes the *most* delicious, 100 percent homemade, organic Christmas cutout cookies in the world. Some Christmases she even grinds her own flour. The only way to have enough baked cookies on hand was for her to start early and freeze them till needed.

When temptation called, I would join my siblings in stealth missions down to the basement to steal cookies. We would inevitably get caught when my mom headed down to the basement to restock the freezer with cookies. Boy did she come upstairs steamed. But really, it was her own fault for making such delicious and tempting cookies!

Rachel: Sean, I have to admit that in my whole life, I have never tasted more delicious Christmas cutout cookies than your mom's. And as hard as we have tried to duplicate her recipe at our home, it never comes close to hers. I officially give up!

Sean: But cookies weren't the only tasty Christmas treats in our house. My Irish grandma Eva's mincemeat pie was another big deal. Growing up, I thought everyone had mincemeat pies at Christmas. The two main ingredients in mincemeat are meat and apples. I know this because my siblings and I used to battle over who would get to grind up the apples and who would grind up the meat. The grinder was the coolest part of the process. As a kid, it was so much fun to watch whole chunks of meat or apples go in one end and a transformed shape and texture come out the other. Using a kind of wooden plunger to push it through made the process even more fun. And when we finished all the hard work, the amazing smell of the spices and cooked apples melded together and wafted through the kitchen and throughout the house. That is truly the smell of Christmas for me. My mom would make pie with the mincemeat, but she also canned some of it so we could spread it on toast and get a little taste and reminder of Christmas later in the year. Unfortunately, since mincemeat is labor-intensive and an acquired taste (i.e., Rachel and the kids aren't huge fans of it) it's one of those Christmas traditions that ended up on the cutting-room floor when we got married.

While our Nativity scene growing up wasn't nearly as big as Rachel's, it still played a central role in our celebration. In my home, the baby Jesus's manger would remain empty until Christmas morning, when one child would be selected to place the figurine into the manger. Being selected to place the baby Jesus in the manger on Christmas morning was a big honor.

On Christmas morning, the kids would get up early, but we knew we could not go down the stairs until our parents were up and ready. Unlike with the cookies, this was a rule we didn't dare break. We'd gather at the top of the stairs and peer down into the predawn half-light, scoping out what was beneath the tree.

Once my parents were up, we all had to sing "Away in a Manger" before we could fly down the stairs to see what Santa had brought us.

Rachel: This is one of the Duffy family traditions we have incorporated into our own family. I just love the patience and anticipation it instills in the kids, and I think singing "Away in a Manger" gives the children one last reminder of the reason for the season before they tear down the stairs to see what gifts St. Nicholas brought them!

Our family's favorite Christmas movie is *White Christmas*. Sean, all the kids, and I love it! I'm sure my love for that classic film has a lot to do with the fact that I am an Arizona girl. It's also why I am forever fascinated with Christmas in Wisconsin, which is always white. Truly, there is nothing like it, especially in the Northwoods, where Sean is from. The giant pine trees of northern Wisconsin make the whole place look like you walked right out of the wardrobe and into the magical world of Narnia.

Sean's hometown, Hayward, is the quaintest, most darling town you have ever seen. When Main Street is decorated with white lights, wreaths, red bows, and of course, lots of snow, it feels like you are living in a Christmas town postcard.

Sean: That's true, Rachel, but we Duffy men would never say "darling." After all, when everyone was home for Christmas, our favorite winter pastime was to go to the local ice rink to play hockey. The men in my sisters' lives would play as well, and so for me, the sounds of Christmas aren't just carols and jingle bells, they are also the slash and scrape of skates across the ice and the thud of a puck off the boards. Hayward is also the home of the world-famous Birkebeiner cross-country ski race. My parents are very athletic and big-time skiers, and my mom is actually the first woman ever to complete the cross-country Worldloppet. She never let having eleven kids slow her down!

Rachel: I'm definitely not as athletic as my mother-in-law, Carol, but I have ice-skated a few times when I was at Sean's family's place. I was always charmed by the stories he'd tell of his mom taking the family to a little pond on a local golf course. The family would skate and Carol brought hot chocolate and hot apple cider to keep them going. They lovingly called it "On Golden Pond." When we were married, I got to join the family for this little tradition. One year the conditions were just right—not too much wind or snow—so that when the pond froze, it was just like glass. It was so transparent that we could see the fish swimming below us.

Sean: That's right, Rachel. And the turtles too. Remember that? Other years growing up, we'd also go to the cabin we owned on a nearby lake. We'd shovel the snow off its surface and play hockey there. We'd have a big bonfire outside on the shore, so if you got cold, or if you were just a spectator, you had a place to keep warm. My mom grew up in a hockey family (her brother Ken Yackel actually played for the US hockey team in the 1952 Olympics), so she'd often join us as we played on the ice. These are some of my fondest Christmas memories.

Rachel: Both of our moms are remarkable women. Like yours, Sean, my mom grew up very poor. Her mom, my grandmother, always seemed to find a way to make Christmas and Three Kings' Day so special for her and her six siblings. My mother often recounts the great sacrifices my grandmother made throughout the year to make it happen. I think that's why my mother took such care to make Christmas magical and beautiful for me and my siblings. As an air force military spouse, she also had a keen sense of the importance of tradition for a family who moved so many times and to so many countries—Spain, Turkey, Peru, England. Having something that we could consistently count on helped us to not feel completely rootless.

Sean: Even though my childhood Christmas experiences are different from Rachel's, we share the idea that family traditions are deeply important—especially for kids.

I'm Irish and Rachel is Hispanic and we grew up thousands and thousands of miles from one another, but interestingly, both of our families share one Christmas-dinner tradition: leg of lamb! For years, Rachel and I carried on the Christmas leg-of-lamb tradition.

Then, the year after I was elected to Congress, we were invited to the annual White House Christmas party. It's such an honor to be invited to the White House and it is never more beautiful than at Christmastime. The decorations are gorgeous—lights, enormous trees, the giant White House gingerbread house with sugar-glass windows, and the traditional White House crèche, or Nativity.

Rachel: The first time we went to the White House Christmas party, we kept pinching ourselves and waiting for someone to scold us for sitting on the couches or putting our wineglasses on the side table. But the best part about the party was the food! The first few years I stuffed my handbag with White House cookies to bring home to the kids. I'm sure with all the security cameras someone saw me do it, but I didn't care. Hands down, though, the most delicious thing served at the White House Christmas party were the lollipop lamb chops. Every year we looked forward to eating the perfectly cooked chops. Eventually it occurred to us that we liked these lamb chops better than leg of lamb, and guess what? They're also easier to make! A double bonus for a busy, huge family like ours. Thus, our family Christmas Eve dinner tradition evolved, and now we enjoy White House–inspired lollipop lamb chops instead of leg of lamb.

Sean: After dinner on Christmas Eve, our kids set up an elaborate Christmas fort, complete with separate "rooms," flashlights, and walkie-talkies, presumably all to see if they can catch Santa in the act of bringing toys. They also include a laptop to watch Christmas movies in the morning as they wait for Mom and Dad to get up. Inevitably, no matter how much we ask them to let us sleep till at least 7 a.m., the kids will come into our room at ungodly hours pleading their case. "Pleeeease!!! We've watched Rudolph already. Please get up. C'mon, please!" The one rule they know not to break is the same rule I never broke when I was a kid—coming downstairs before Mom and Dad are ready with camera and coffee in hand to capture all the memories.

Rachel: And just like in Sean's family, we make our kids sit on the stairs and sing "Away in a Manger" before they can come downstairs and find their gifts under the tree.

Sean: Even before we had a ton of kids, it was never a free-for-all. They find the gifts with their name on them and create a personal pile. Then, starting from youngest to oldest, we let everyone open a present in turn, one by one. This serves two purposes: it lets the joy and anticipation linger and it avoids mass pandemonium and mess.

Rachel: As you can imagine, with so many kids, opening one gift at a time, our Christmas-morning gift unwrapping lasts for several hours—and we wouldn't have it any other way! It's so fun to sit in our pajamas, drinking coffee and watching our kids receive their gifts and be genuinely excited to see what Santa brought their siblings too.

This past year was a real reminder that life has many uncertainties. None of us could have predicted a pandemic in our futures, and we all had our world rocked by it. In November 2020, COVID hit Wisconsin really hard. Our whole family, including Sean's parents and virtually all of his siblings and their families, came down with the virus. Luckily, everyone survived it well and Sean and I decided that getting COVID before Christmas was a blessing. With COVID behind us and our bodies now filled with antibodies, we felt much safer about my parents traveling from Arizona to spend a month with us—Christmas through Epiphany. After so many months on lockdown in their Scottsdale condo, they were never more excited to embrace the crazy, chaotic Duffy household.

Sean: The second Christmas miracle came from what was a real disappointment. For more than a quarter century, the entire Duffy family—my mom, dad, ten siblings, and their spouses—had a long-standing tradition of attending the Wassail Luncheon Concert in Bayfield, Wisconsin. It happens annually at a beautiful restored Victorian mansion called the Old Rittenhouse Inn. The Rittenhouse re-creates an old English Christmas in decorations, food, and music. In addition to a flaming figgy pudding and many other Victorian touches, the most amazing choral singers in all of northern Wisconsin serenade you throughout your meal with traditional English Christmas carols, some of which are being forgotten. It's hard to describe how festive and awesome this annual event and Duffy tradition is, and suffice it to say we look forward to it all year long because simply nothing compares to how much it puts you in good cheer and in the Christmas spirit.

Rachel: Well, with the pandemic, it was canceled, and for the first time in twenty-five years, the Duffys would not be gathering for the occasion. However, Sean's siblings decided that they were not going to let this dampen their cheer. They decided to re-create the Wassail meal at Sean's parents' home. The owner who runs the Rittenhouse heard we were carrying on the tradition and sent over a few jars of the delicious homemade jams they serve. We made a playlist from the Rittenhouse Wassail album, now on iTunes, and my brother and sister-in-law

Brian and Holly took the lead by helping to organize and divide up the work. I was given the task of making a figgy pudding soaked in enough brandy that it could easily be flamed at the end of our delicious meal! You probably won't be surprised to hear that the 2020 Christmas Wassail was by far the best, most raucous, and most fun Wassail in twenty-five years! And the bonus blessing is that for the first time since Sean and I were married, my parents finally got the chance to experience the Wassail—not at the fancy Rittenhouse Victorian mansion, but in the warmth and glow of the home Sean grew up in.

Sean: COVID or no COVID, there are always things that come along to surprise us during the holidays. Sometimes those things delight us, and sometimes they try us. So having things we can count on at Christmas makes us feel and believe that no matter what else comes our way, we've got people and things we can rely on.

Rachel: God gave us the greatest gift the world has ever received. Each year we mark that amazing, miraculous gift of love by celebrating Jesus's birth and our own salvation through this tiny baby prince of peace.

Sean: What I love about what Rachel and I have done, what so many married couples do, is to join together parts of both our pasts to create a new present. From that union we help shape how our kids will remember and celebrate Christmas long into the future and long after we are gone.

Rachel: The one thread that runs through all of our lives, and not just at Christmas, is family. Jesus chose to be born into a family, and Sean and I are so blessed to have a large family and be part of an even bigger family—God's family.

At Christmas, we welcome Jesus into our lives and our homes. We welcome family and friends. We could say that they are guests, but they are far more than that. They are a part of who we are and how we came to be so blessed and so grateful for all we've been given.

Sean: As the saying goes, "The more the merrier." On Christmas Day, after we pick up all the wrapping paper, and the kids play with their toys, and Rachel and I recover with a little catnap, we gather again to have a little birthday party for Jesus.

Rachel: I light the candles on the decorated birthday cake and we all sing "Happy Birthday" to Jesus—the reason for the season. As our family grows, the merrier our Christmas gets. Thank you, Jesus, for the gift of family. And merry Christmas to you, our FOX News Family!

Rachel Campos-Duffy serves as a cohost of *FOX & Friends Weekend*.

Sean Duffy serves as a FOX News Media contributor.

The
Joy of
Family

Janice Dean

For Janice Dean, Christmas means remembering her childhood in Canada—from maple syrup to Boxing Day. The journey home reminds her why it's important to never forget your roots.

I've lived in the United States for the last twenty years, but my earliest memories of Christmas are of the time I spent in my native Canada. I think it's important that we don't forget where we come from—both literally and figuratively. As a result, I also think it's important to know where your traditions come from. For example, I grew up in Ottawa, Canada's capital city, which has both British and French influences. Ottawa is in the province of Ontario, with the province of Quebec right next door to us, which is completely French. In school, our secondary language is French, and most children are encouraged to

Janice Dean and her mom.

speak both English and French. It's very difficult to work in Ottawa without being bilingual.

Canada's government is heavily influenced by the British parliament and an elected prime minister. Our head of state is still the Queen of England. She is on all of our dollar bills and coins. When I was growing up in the capital city, many of my school trips were to see the Parliament Buildings in the heart of downtown Ottawa.

British influences are in many of our traditions, including several of our holidays. The day after Christmas, December 26, is called Boxing Day. It comes from the custom of "Christmas boxes," gifts of money or goods given to the less fortunate. It's also another opportunity, since it is another day off from work, for families to get together.

I remember that growing up we would listen on the radio or watch on television Queen Elizabeth II giving her yearly Christmas broadcast. And during our big Christmas meal, we would each have a Christmas cracker to open. They aren't something you eat; rather, they are tubes wrapped in festive paper that make a loud snapping sound when pulled open, and often contain a small gift and a joke. As kids we would be a bit scared to open the tabs because of how loud the noise could be. But it was always fun to see the little toy, paper hat, or written message inside, so it would be worth the ear-popping *snap*.

Did you know that Canada produces 71 percent of the world's pure maple syrup? And 91 percent of it is produced in Quebec. Canada's maple syrup–producing regions are located in the provinces of Quebec (primary producer), Ontario, New Brunswick, Prince Edward Island, and Nova Scotia. Growing up, I didn't realize how special this fact was, but now that I'm older, I have a big appreciation for maple syrup. So much so that when I go back home, I always bring a big crate of it back to New York to give as gifts to friends at Christmas.

Every spring as kids we'd drive out to a sugar bush, an area where maple trees grow and syrup is tapped from them and processed. I have so many memories of going there with my family or on school trips when there would be a "sugar shack" at the end of the trip where the fresh maple syrup could be sampled on the snow.

For me, an indication of the approach of the holiday season was my mother taking out her favorite festive Christmas sweaters. Stella, my mom, firmly believes that she is the one who began what is now known in the US as the "ugly Christmas sweater" tradition. Now, you have to understand that my mother doesn't believe that the sweaters she wears for the season are ugly. They're just beautiful Christmas-themed garments. I have photographic evidence dating back to when I was in my late teens or early twenties of her wearing her Christmas sweaters. She's joined me on *FOX & Friends* several times when I've donned my "ugly Christmas sweater," but she'll always correct me and say it's not ugly. Christmas sweaters are always beautiful, and the more festive the better. Most anything related to Christmas is special.

One other favorite Canadian tradition I remember from when I was younger is my mother making a dessert that originated in British Columbia called Nanaimo bars. They're named for the coastal city in that province on the Pacific side of the country. Even just saying their name makes my mouth water. They are delicious three-layered bars (some call them squares) that have a crumb base, a chocolate crumb base, and incredibly yummy custard-flavored icing in the middle, with thick chocolate fudge on top. My mom makes the best Nanaimo bars, and I am reminded of her and Christmas whenever I think of them.

Nanaimo Bars

1 cup graham cracker crumbs
½ cup sweetened flaked coconut
½ cup sweetened shredded coconut
⅓ cup walnuts, finely chopped

¼ cup cocoa powder
¼ cup granulated sugar
⅓ cup butter, melted
1 egg, lightly beaten

Filling

¼ cup (½ stick) softened butter
2 tablespoons custard powder
½ teaspoon vanilla

2 cups icing sugar
2 tablespoons milk

Topping

4 ounces semisweet chocolate, chopped   1 tablespoon butter

1. Preheat the oven to 350°F. Line a 9-inch square metal cake pan with parchment paper.

2. In a medium bowl, stir together the graham cracker crumbs, flaked and shredded coconut, walnuts, cocoa powder, and sugar. Drizzle with the butter and egg, and stir until combined. Press the crumb mixture into the prepared cake pan. Bake until firm, about 10 minutes. Let cool in the pan on a wire rack.

3. **Filling:** In a medium bowl, beat together the butter, custard powder, and vanilla. Beat in the icing sugar alternately with the milk until smooth, adding up to 1 teaspoon more milk if the mixture is too thick to spread. Spread over the cooled base and refrigerate until firm, about 1 hour.

4. **Topping:** In a heatproof bowl over a saucepan of hot (not boiling) water, melt the chocolate with the butter. Spread over the filling and refrigerate until almost set, about 30 minutes.

5. With the tip of a knife, score into bars; refrigerate until chocolate is set, about 1 hour. (Make ahead: Wrap and refrigerate for up to 4 days or overwrap in heavy-duty foil and freeze for up to 2 weeks.) Cut into bars.

Even though I've been in the United States all these years, like many people, a big part of celebrating Christmas is making the trip back home. That time of the year always stirs up a lot of memories of Christmas in my homeland and, like it is for many people who live in northern latitudes, involves plenty of cold and snow. Ottawa, the city I grew up in, is known as one of the coldest capitals in the world and is also famous for having the world's longest outdoor skating rink!

The Rideau Canal Skateway is 7.8 kilometers (4.8 miles) long and has a total maintained surface area of 165,621 square meters (1.782 million square feet), which is equivalent to ninety Olympic-size skating rinks! I have skated the canal for many years and it's one of my favorite things to do in the winter back home.

I think it's important to remember where you come from for a lot of reasons, but perhaps the most relevant one is how much it reminds us of the lessons and wisdom we learned in the past. As time goes by, it's easy to get swept up in events and forget to be grateful for our blessings and to recall the wisdom we've built up over time. Memory is one method of time travel, so we might as well use it!

Another way of time traveling is watching my kids repeat the things I did when I was growing up. I am thrilled when my kids get to do winter activities around the holidays. My youngest, Theodore, actually learned how to skate a few winters ago when we visited my mom in London, Ontario, the city just outside of Toronto where she lives now.

Speaking of Theodore, last year he created a poster of his favorite Christmas traditions and other things we do as a family. It was fun for him to choose the things that mattered to him most during this special time of year, including trips to see Santa. I have shown my kids the many photographs I still have of me visiting Santa Claus. One particular time I remember well was when I was about five years old, and I was called to receive my gift from Santa. I had a half-eaten lollipop in my hand. Santa presented me with the gift, and as he leaned over, the lollipop met the fuzzy beard. I noticed right away that the beard hair wasn't normal hair. I remember thinking about that, and the photo shows me looking at him and that lollipop stuck on the white fuzzy beard. There's clearly a shadow of a doubt in my expression. It took a few more years, after I started school, for the Santa story to completely unravel. I was at the bus stop one day and an older boy named Bruce ruined the magic of Santa. I was really, really upset.

I never told my mom and dad that I knew the truth. But perhaps that was the beginning of my career in journalism, because I did do some investigative reporting. One year I started to look around the house to see if I could find where my parents were hiding the gifts. I searched through their bedroom closet, and I found them. Wrapped up. That didn't stop me, though. I did some further examination of the facts and opened one of the gifts. I was very careful about it and able to forensically reseal it, keeping the tape intact. I remember being both delighted and horrified by what I'd done. "Oh, this is terrible!" and "Oh, YAY! I got what I wanted!"

Of course, as a parent you want to preserve the Santa magic as long as you can. It's such a great part of childhood and innocence. Theodore still believes, but my older child, Matthew, came to me one day saying his friends were telling him there was no Santa Claus. Matthew didn't know what to believe, but for a while I was able to convince him by saying that I still believe in Santa. Finally, about two years ago, that ended. He said to me, "Is it true that you and Dad are Santa Claus?"

I asked him if he really, really wanted to know the truth. He said he did. Afterward, he was clearly upset by what I'd told him. The great thing was, though, that once he settled down, he said to me, "Well, let's not tell Theodore." I loved that he wanted his younger brother to have that belief and that magic.

One of my favorite ways to keep that sentiment alive is by reading to the boys on Christmas Eve. I still have the copy of *The Night Before Christmas* that I had as a child. So every year, my husband and I get that out and read it to them. That's a special part of the night, and I hope someday they'll do the same with their families. I've never looked on going back home as anything but a joy. I feel wonderful when we pack up the car and head up to London, Ontario, to see my mother—

their grandmother Stella—and some of my extended family. I still love getting up on Christmas morning and watching the kids open their presents at their grandmother's house. Like it was for so many people, this past Christmas was the first time the kids didn't get to go to Grandma's house because of the pandemic. That was difficult and sad, but we're hopeful we'll make the trip again this year.

While putting up our tree and unpacking all our decorations, I do get a sense of being home. I still have the angel that my mother and father used on their tree for many years. It has to be at least seventy years old now. It was always a delicate object and is even more so now after all this time. We don't put it on the tree for fear of it getting damaged, but just seeing it brings back so many memories. I picture my mom in the kitchen preparing food and storing it in containers to go into the freezer. She works for weeks before Christmas Day to make sure that all our favorite things are there when we arrive. I'm smiling now as I think of going to see my aunt Janet and uncle Ian in my cousin Tracy's home. In that memory they're sitting around the dinner table with silver spoons balanced on their noses. Everyone on my mother's side of the family has that special talent. I also hear the sound of us playing "music" using Aunt Janet's fine crystal glasses. We wet the rims and run our fingers around them. My kids were in awe of how you could do this and always try to do it on our glasses at home, but we keep reminding them it has to be the fancy crystal to get that pretty ringing sound.

The smell of a turkey roasting in the oven has a special additional scent memory. My mom is from Newfoundland, a province on the eastern, Atlantic side of Canada. She stuffs the turkey and adds a special blend of spices that Newfoundlanders use. What's in it I can't tell you. It's a secret I have never been let in on. I suppose that's a good thing, because truth be told, I'm a terrible cook and I've never made a meal for a large group of people. Thank God my husband, Sean, took over those duties this past year when we weren't able to get home to Canada for Christmas. Sean's a firefighter and has had hundreds of tours making big meals for many people in the last two decades, so he has a talent that I do not.

The kids benefit from his job as a proud member of the FDNY as well. At every firehouse Sean has served out of, they've hosted a Christmas party for the families. The kids love his old fire station on Great Jones Street, where the main event is seeing Santa and a couple of his reindeer being "rescued" from the top of a building. Several of the firefighters climb up on the tower ladder and escort Old Saint Nick to safety. He then gets out of the tower ladder and heads into the firehouse to distribute gifts. It's a big tradition within the New York City firefighting community, and we look forward to that party as another example of their fellowship and spirit of giving.

For Sean and me, Christmas is even more special. Our first date was on December 18, 2002. I had just moved to New York and I had mentioned to him that I wanted to come into Manhattan to see the Christmas tree at Rockefeller Center. I drove across the Fifty-Ninth Street Bridge after my morning shift, and he was just getting off a "24" (a day-and-night tour). It was my very first time seeing the tree, and we had breakfast at a diner afterward right near St. Patrick's Cathedral. Every year we go as a family to see the tree, and last year when Theodore put together his favorite Christmas traditions poster for school, going to see the tree at Rockefeller Center was featured prominently on it.

In spite of all the bad things that COVID brought us, our family did institute a new tradition this year. My boys are very talented musicians. They each play cello and piano. We shared the gift of a Christmas concert via Zoom for the family—in both Canada and the US. Matthew and Theodore played for all the relatives. They did traditional Christmas songs and even a few classical pieces that were suitable for the season. Whether live or via the internet, we're going to continue to share music with family from now on.

Speaking of music, for many years when I started my career in broadcasting, I worked as a classic-rock deejay, so I combined my love of traditional Christmas carols—"O Come, All Ye Faithful" is a particular favorite—with classic Bing

Janice in a Christmas sweater.

Crosby renditions and the Eagles and Don Henley's version of "Please Come Home for Christmas." Bono and U2 covered that same song, and there's Bob Geldof with one of my favorite Christmas originals, Band Aid, featuring all the famous rock and pop singers of the eighties, singing "Do They Know It's Christmas?" to help support famine relief. Bruce Springsteen and "Santa Claus Is Comin' to Town" has to be included in there. Those are fun to mix into any playlist for Christmas. Like all forms of music, Christmas tunes can suit your mood.

Those rock versions, especially, bring back some great memories of the times when I was a deejay. Because I was single, I'd volunteer to do the overnight shift on Christmas Eve. I was in my twenties and didn't have a family of my own, so I wanted the other deejays to be with theirs. I loved it, actually. It wasn't a sad or lonely time. I'd be in the darkened studio with a few strings of Christmas lights on. Between songs, I'd take calls from listeners. They'd make requests and share with me what was going on at their houses—decorating their tree, sipping eggnog, having a big party or a quiet night with family. A few people who called in were looking for company and comfort. For those who were by themselves or working like I was, having someone to talk to, someone to share the experience of being alone, was important to them. I loved the idea of reaching out that way, being a part of their lives for even just a few moments while we chatted, and then playing a song that would bring them comfort and joy.

I also loved it when people from my past, former classmates or coworkers, would call in to say hello and wish me a merry Christmas. It's wonderful how a voice going out over the airwaves or on a phone line could connect people and bring them close. The radio station also used to do various charity events around Christmas, and it felt so good as employees of the station to join with the listeners and help others. In Canada, an organization known as the Snowsuit Fund provides warm clothes for kids in need. I am also reminded of the Salvation Army in Canada. Like their counterparts in the US, they were a big part of the holiday season, with their bell ringers and their bands playing on street corners or outside stores. At the various radio stations and TV stations I worked at, we often raised money for the Salvation Army and its efforts to relieve people's burdens around this time of year.

I'm sure you've noticed that as the meteorologist on *FOX & Friends*, I enjoy performing in front of a crowd. When I was younger, I sang in the choir at school and acted in plays. I always loved the Christmas concerts and getting dressed up for them. One year, I got to combine all my favorite things. I was the narrator who read *The Night Before Christmas* while the rest of the cast acted out the scenes. That was a big deal for me and strengthened my connection to that classic story. I also went door-to-door caroling and loved sharing the gift of music and the spirit of the season along the way.

For me, Christmas is about connecting and sharing. As December approaches, I'm busy preparing our yearly family card. I put together a series of photos of the key events that happened during the year. I really enjoy doing it. It gives me a chance to reflect, remember, and share, and be grateful for the many blessings my family has received. That's what Christmas should do for us. It is the celebration of the birth of Jesus, and we want to spread the message of the good news of Him coming to us all with His hopeful message of love. In ways large and small, sharing meals and memories, listening to favorite songs, doing good works, we spread that important message. It doesn't matter where we're from or where we now live or what kind of sweater we wear, for me, Christmas is such a magical time of year.

So from my family to yours, merry Christmas!

. . . And may you never be too grown-up to search the skies on Christmas Eve . . .

Janice Dean currently serves as a senior meteorologist for FOX News Channel and morning meteorologist for *FOX & Friends* (weekdays 6–9 a.m. ET).

Steve and Peter
Doocy

*Steve and Peter Doocy recall memories of Christmases past, from
Steve's commitment to capturing memories on tape to Peter's
encounter with Santa in a very surprising spot in New York City.*

Steve: Sometime in 1987, when my wife, Kathy, was pregnant with our son, Peter, I saw a story that set me on a path I hadn't considered taking before. This gentleman had been snapping a photo of his son on the young man's birthday for twenty-five consecutive years. More than that, he took the photo with his son standing in the exact same spot every time. It was a time-lapse family, every shot taken one year later. I know that has been done by millions of parents by now, but this was the first I'd heard of it. I didn't want to copy his idea

The Doocy family.

exactly, but I liked the concept of having that year-to-year record we could all review at some point in the future.

I decided then and there that I wanted to video our children coming down the stairs on Christmas morning to get to the tree and the presents beneath it. So, the first Christmas that Peter could walk on his own, we instituted what has become an ongoing tradition. Mary, our second child, joined us in time for the second year of the photo opportunity and was carried downstairs by my wife, Kathy, and then our youngest child, Sally, joined her brother and sister for the mad dash down the stairs, a cherished family tradition that we kept alive every single year after that, right up until the 2020 pandemic, which kept Peter from joining us at the home he'd grown up in.

Some of you reading this may have seen a collection of clips that I stitched together into a video that we aired on *FOX & Friends* about fifteen years ago. Quite a few times, Kathy and I have been out at a promotional event for one of my books or some other function, and, inevitably, someone will approach us and say, "Hey! I watched your kids grow up running down the stairs."

I'm glad that treasured family moment, and such an iconic experience in many kids' lives, has been one we can share. After all, that's what Christmas is all about: giving. Right, Peter?

Peter: That's true, Dad. From my perspective, though, as kids we might not have been as charitable and loving as the season calls for. At the top of the steps, we did engage in some jostling to get to the head of the line and be the first one down the stairs and to that tree. It was almost as if we were basketball players trying to box out our opponent and get the rebound!

Steve: Peter's right; the competition was fierce. It took Mary twenty-eight years to finally get to the tree first, and she celebrated with a little end-zone dance. Peter dominated the competition for most of those years.

Peter: Dad should know all about it. As the cameraman/director, he wanted to be sure he got as much of the moment on tape as possible. He was like a cameraman at a NASCAR race filming us as we dashed past him, banked the turn through the dining room, and then the straightaway through the kitchen to get to the tree.

Steve: Christmas morning wasn't always easy on Kathy and me. Like most kids, our three were so eager to see what Santa had brought that they'd wake us up at 4 a.m. Sorry, kids, that's a little too early. Seven thirty arrived too soon for me. The kids would be sitting at the top of the steps. We'd edge around them, get the coffeepot going, turn on the lights of the tree, and then yell, "Okay! Santa was here!"

Some of those Christmas mornings came especially quickly since I was often up the night before Christmas and all through the house assembling one gift or another. Despite missing or lost pieces, I always managed to get everything together thanks to duct tape. If it was good enough for NASA engineers, it was good enough for me. I also enlisted the aid of our neighbor Ed to carry larger, bulkier items into the basement. One year he was especially valuable because we'd purchased an air hockey table. Assembly wasn't the issue; it was how to fit an object that was only about one-sixteenth of an inch narrower than the stairwell. We managed. The kids shouted in delight when they saw it, and to that point, that was the loudest I'd ever heard Peter shriek, which made all the efforts worthwhile.

Peter: That gift was a complete surprise, and I knew that it had to have come from Santa because it must have taken a bit of magic to get into place in that basement. It is still down there, along with tons of memories of Christmases past that live down there with it. I know that Dad has tried a few times to clean up the assorted things collected down there, but my sisters and I are resistant to having anything purged from the collection—we have so many memories attached to what's stored down there.

Steve: I've talked to other parents, and they mention getting rid of some of their kids' things. I could never do that. Our basement is like the kids' National Archives. Our house outside New York City still looks like they left the house fifteen minutes ago and not the fifteen years it's been since Peter moved away.

Part of the reason why we are such keepers is that I don't have a single toy from my childhood. I have to be honest here and say that we were poor. I remember when my dad came home from serving in the military in Germany; he brought me a stuffed tiger. One of my sisters tore the head off the thing. That makes elbowing at the top of the stairs seem pretty mild, but I kept that one toy for a long, long time. It wasn't a Christmas present, but it still meant a lot to me, and as a result, I wanted to be sure to preserve as much of our kids' Christmas memories as possible.

I do have one memory, thanks to a photograph depicting the scene, of me at age four with a tea set that my mom and I would play with. It was what they could afford at Christmas, and I knew that money was tight, so whatever they got us was something to be grateful for. As a result of that modest upbringing, Kathy and I always tried to keep things in perspective for our kids. We didn't buy anything too extravagant or over-the-top and kept the emphasis on that tried-and-trusted truth about it being the thought that counts.

Over time we instituted two rules. The first was that the kids had to wrap themselves any gifts they bought for us or for one another. No gift bags! That's too easy. Put some thought and effort into every part of the gift. Second, we asked that they not purchase cards; instead, we asked them to write a poem or a story from their own imaginations. Peter was very good at coming up with difficult rhymes, and all the kids would incorporate events from the previous year as part of the plot or part of the poem. Kathy and I believe in practicing what we preach, so for our birthdays, we adhere to the same rules. The kids added to the tradition by doing the same thing—wrapping and writing original pieces—for our birthdays as well as Mother's Day and Father's Day.

Those are all happy Christmas memories and they help take some of the sting out of a less-pleasant one. In 1997, my mother died on Christmas morning. That reframed Christmas for me. You look forward to Christmas all year and you remember all the great things about the day. Then, halfway through Christmas every year now, I'll stop and think, "This is the day my mom died."

Then I'll think, "Okay, happy day, worst day."

Like so many things in life, it's complicated.

Her death also brings to mind when I was growing up in Salina, Kansas. We'd have a big turkey dinner at Thanksgiving. We'd all be in a food fog, but Dad would jingle the car keys and all of us—I've got four sisters—would pile into the car. We'd drive over to Country Club Plaza, and we'd tour through that nice neighborhood with all the big houses and admire and appreciate the elaborate decorations. That was the sign that the holiday season was upon us. After Thanksgiving, I'm good with Christmas music; before that it seems too much like we're rushing things together.

Peter: Dad has to remember "the ladder." He would drag that thing out of the garage, and maybe this is just my childhood imagination, but it had to be thirty to forty feet tall. Well, okay, I can see that Dad's signaling that it was thirty-two, but he would use that ladder to assist him in hanging lights on the outside of the house. Even when I was really young, I was enlisted as the ladder holder as Dad tried to diagnose why not all of the bulbs would light.

Steve: As I got older, and after Kathy heard about some well-known person getting injured taking down the lights, she forbade me from going up and down the ladder. At first she was okay with me taking them down four or five months later when there wasn't snow or ice to contend with. I remember telling our neighbor J.R., when he asked about them still being up so long after the holiday, that they were our Christmas lights, but now they are our Lent lights. Things change so much—now our house is partly illuminated by lasers from the neighbor's house! Some things have to change with the times, I suppose, but we still have strings of bulbs somewhere in the basement in a box next to the air hockey table. The best of both worlds.

I'm a former president of the Future Farmers of America at Clay Center High School. I've always been a supporter of natural Christmas trees. Up until five years ago, we always had one. Then, while adjusting the tree to make sure it was straight, a frog jumped out of the tree. The sight of it was so shocking to Kathy, along with the story a neighbor told about their tree being infested with termites, that we decided that too much nature indoors wasn't a good thing either. I still miss the real Christmas tree smell, though.

Sometimes you make a change and sometimes change is forced upon you. In the early years of our marriage, Kathy and I decorated the tree in our house in Virginia with family heirloom ornaments. They were quite lovely and, as you'd expect, brought back lots of memories. One year, when Mary was still a toddler, she pulled on the tree and it came tumbling down, shattering a bunch of the irreplaceable ornaments. One did survive, and we still put it on the tree. Kathy and I honeymooned in Hawaii, and we bought a Christmas ornament while there. It was like an envelope and had some blue water in it and sand and shells. It's completely dried out now, but we still put it up, and it still brings back great memories.

Peter: I was in the other room when that tree fell. And, in Mary's defense, I think it might have fallen because of where and how it was positioned. Although, at the time, I wondered if it was because Mary and I had been dancing around it to "Rockin' Around the Christmas Tree." We may have literally rocked it off balance. To us, the words were less like lyrics and more like instructions.

Your talking about getting older points out something that's important for me to say, Dad. I think that it took me going away to college to really appreciate one of the best aspects of Christmas—the food. One of the other great traditions we have is baking gingerbread cookies. Mom waits until we're all home before she mixes the dough and bakes them from scratch. She also makes different-colored icing and puts it in piping bags so that we can decorate the cookies. We draw things, write things out, make shapes, outline a face. My sisters and I sit there with Mom, and we talk and laugh and compare our creations. Of course, just like with the stairs, we have to be competitive. You want to be the one who made the best-looking cookie.

In addition to that, the older that I get, the more I appreciate all the months in advance that my mom spends thinking about practical gifts or things she wants to cook for everybody or things we should do when we're all together. Now that I am more of an adult, I realize that that takes a lot of time and a lot of thought and a lot of effort, and it adds to the whole good feeling of the season when you realize how much goes into it. It's never just getting everybody together. There is a mother who puts a lot of thought into it ahead of time.

Steve: Absolutely, and I really enjoy watching the kids do the gingerbread cookie decorating. It's fun to see them come to the table looking like adults and being transformed into kids again. They haven't seen one another for a while, and even though they have all the responsibilities of independent adults, I love seeing them back in that "I'm a seven-year-old kid again" mode. And, truth be told, they sometimes take liberties with the decorating and some of those gingerbread men taste good and are good for a laugh too.

Kathy's determined that our children still get to have all those moments and memories. A few years ago she had to have a series of knee surgeries after being knocked down by our golden retriever. I can still picture her in the kitchen during that rough period of rehabilitation, on crutches and with her knee in a huge brace, her leg throbbing, and she was leaning up against the center island mixing that dough. She wasn't about to buy premade dough or cookies. She knew what was important to her kids and she never let them down.

Peter: The two of you always supported us. I remember elementary school and middle school and us participating in a holiday music festival. The kids who were in the band or the orchestra would play. I was in the chorus, so I sang. We learned religious and secular Christmas songs and carols. Everybody's parents showed up on the nights of the performances and it was all a lot of fun.

Steve: That reminds me of the Christmas pageant at the church. Peter, you were a king. Mary was a Wise Man, and Sally, our youngest, was the Christmas dog. I remember thinking, "Wait! There's no Christmas dog!" I should know. I serve as lector at our Catholic church and I've had the privilege of reading the accounts of Christmas from Matthew and Luke to the congregation. I don't remember any mention of Fido. No matter, the story of the Christ child is always an important part of our faith and our celebration during the season.

Another part of our celebration is watching an updated version of Charles Dickens's *A Christmas Carol*. I'm talking about, of course, Bill Murray starring in *Scrooged*. It has all the elements of the original, the Ghosts of Christmas Past and Christmas Present, but it's set in a more contemporary time. It's fun now to remember the eighties with people and their big hair. I enjoy watching Robert Mitchum in it. But the message still comes through: the impact we can have on people's lives, how we can change, what the spirit of giving means. We all like to watch that together, and when, at the end, Murray sings "Put a Little Love in Your Heart," we all get up and sing and dance. Now that the kids are older and we're enjoying a drink or two while watching it, we turn up the volume a bit and the dancing gets a bit freer. No trees have tumbled as a result, but we're rocking near the Christmas tree.

We also love the *Home Alone* movies and we have a somewhat unusual connection to that movie.

Peter: I know what you're about to say, Dad. John Hughes wrote those movies, and he also produced a remake of *Miracle on 34th Street*. I was still pretty young, and you got an invitation to go to a premiere or an early screening.

Steve: That's right. We were running a bit late and hustled you kids into the next-to-last row. This was at the Ziegfeld Theatre in Manhattan. Behind us sat John Hughes himself. At the end of the movie, he tapped me on the shoulder and said, "I watched your son the entire movie to see if he laughed in the right places." I asked him, "Did he?" He said, "Absolutely." And I thought, "Well, isn't that nice? Peter Doocy is a one-person focus group for the most successful movie-comedy writer-director in history."

After the movie, we went to the Sea Grill at Rockefeller Center for an after party with the cast and crew. Peter, why don't you pick up the story from there?

Peter: I was a little kid, and after all that time watching the movie, I had to go to the bathroom. As I was standing there, a man with a white beard came up to the urinal next to me. It was Santa Claus! Well, it was Richard Attenborough, who played Santa in the film. We still talk about that and laugh. Imagine a kid who still believed in Santa seeing that! Not only was Santa out of uniform but . . .

Steve: You know, I've been very fortunate in my career, and we've been able to enjoy attending events like that as a result. We've also, and now Peter does as well since he's working at FOX News, attended the White House Christmas party. We also collect the White House Christmas ornaments. The party is a beautiful scene with the official White House Christmas tree, wonderful food is served, and I've met the Obamas there and the Bush family. It's all very nice, but when you get right down to it, Christmas is about being at home with your own family. We've been fortunate to be able to do that for so many years. My family was in Kansas and Kathy's is from California, and often because of work, and by choice, we spent Christmas at our home, just the five of us. Now the kids are getting married, we've some new faces around the table, and that's wonderful too. You don't have to be at the White House. You can be at your house. And being together is the magic of Christmas.

Steve Doocy currently serves as the cohost of *FOX & Friends* (weekdays 6–9 a.m. ET).

Peter Doocy currently serves as a White House correspondent for FOX News Channel.

Bill Hemmer

Bill Hemmer explains how Christmas wouldn't be Christmas without the satisfied feeling of being at home with family.

Like it is for most people, Christmas for me is about family and being at home in Ohio. For most of my adult life, I've lived away for my job, but I've had the good fortune of making it back to Cincinnati, Ohio, for Christmas. It is a special aspect of life that I have both parents together at Christmas along with my five siblings. And I have an entire litter of nieces and nephews— eleven of them now—and today they are having kids, which makes me a great-uncle. Twice now. Our house gets loud. Festive too, but loud. I know my parents love to have the crowd around them; after all, it is what we grew up with. Just like my folks, I have fond memories of my grandparents George and Helen Knittle.

*Bill Hemmer (front right, in stripes), with siblings
(from left) Tracy, Ann, Andy, and (middle) Kris.*

(The *K* is silent, but they were not.) They really loved to cook a giant Christmas brunch and have us over on Christmas Day.

We called my grandmother DeeDee. She would prepare an enormous spread for us all, and I know it would take days to make all the food. We would eat so much, a food coma was inevitable and all of us would end up lying down on their carpet. Comatose. My grandmother had certain dishes—like sugar cookies—

that were her specialty. Today, my sisters carry on her traditions, and they bring back memories of my grandparents.

My grandfather George Knittle lived to be one hundred years old. For the last three years of his life, he lived at a senior facility called Bayley. Imagine being ninety-seven years old and transitioning to a new residence. Well, Papa did it with real ease and grace. He embraced the staff and they embraced him. He had a real winning way with people and I know he left a real impression. He befriended everyone, and I know he was grateful to spend his final years there. To honor his memory and to thank the staff, I helped organize a charity golf tournament. We're coming up on nearly twenty years for the event, and we are eager to see it resume after a COVID-related hiatus.

Although Papa's name is on the tournament—the George Knittle Memorial is the title of the event—he serves as a representative for so many others who have a relationship with and have benefited from Bayley. Papa's experience allows you to see that facilities like Bayley are more than just buildings; they're communities of people. The way to measure the quality of life is through social interactions, and Papa was a shining example of someone who always reached out to others. The golf tournament is similar in how it reaches others. Not only does it introduce people to what the facility offers but it also serves as a means to raise funds for seniors who can't pay their bills. I'm honored that I can give back and pay tribute to my grandfather and to serve his memory. He, along with grandmother and my parents, were always remarkably generous, and not just at Christmas. I grew up in a Catholic home and attended parochial schools, and the message of giving and being of service was deeply ingrained in both environments.

As a kid, celebrating at home was important, but we had a second Christmas to look forward to with our grandparents. It was wonderful to see how much joy and love the act of giving produced in them. They experienced the same sense of anticipation in the lead-up to Christmas as we did. Sharing those moments with the whole family was really what Christmas was all about. Any time we went to see them, we were all so happy. Christmas helped shine a brighter light on that happiness and made stronger memories over time.

Like most families, we had traditions. My family would tour the neighborhood trying to find the best outdoor decorations. There was some grand competition. I'm one of five kids, so packing us into our station wagon made for tight quarters, and we'd often jostle for space. "Don't act squished," we'd joke. We were good kids for the most part, and on those Christmas Eve tours, we were well aware, if not always mindful, of the naughty-and-nice equation.

That drive and stroll through the neighborhood was the bookend at the beginning of our holiday celebration while the meal at our grandparents' was the other.

In between, we would hold a gift exchange that we called Kriss Kringle. It was the culmination of a month-long campaign of deception and deceit. The extended family drew names at Thanksgiving to determine the person for whom they would be purchasing a gift. It was nearly as much fun engaging in acts of subterfuge to confuse the other parties about the identity of the person you'd chosen as it was buying the gift itself. We have expanded our exchange to include the newest members of the family, and now there are various versions of the Kriss Kringle gift exchange. That's when the house gets loud again.

As a boy, I was pretty typical—army men and race cars seemed to be pretty popular in my memory. My parents were as generous as possible and would make sure the day was special. As an adult, one Christmas was spent in Kandahar, Afghanistan, in the months after 9/11. This was just as the global war on terror was beginning. The US military set up its initial footprint at the airport in Kandahar and I was dispatched to report on it. Seeing those service personnel—members of Special Forces units like the Navy SEALs and Army Rangers, and other agencies like the CIA and FBI—at Christmastime was revealing. I did not serve, but I got to know these individuals and hear their stories and share with them the experience of being away from home at Christmas. It was a rewarding assignment, and

I got to know our service members as husbands and fathers, brothers and sons, wives, sisters and daughters. My level of respect for them as people was forever etched in my mind. Seeing the sacrifices they made was a significant experience for me. Ordinary people doing extraordinary things in service of their country is an act of gift giving that none of us should take for granted.

I also don't take for granted the relationships I have with my brothers and sisters and their children. I've developed close relationships with my nieces and nephews. I try to meet them at their level, whether they're in the sixth grade—still impressionable—or in their early thirties with kids of their own. As an uncle, you can develop an open and often different relationship with an adult relative who isn't their mom or dad. I would not say the relationship is better or more important. But it's different. I think I can help in other ways—listening, guiding, mentoring. I can share with them aspects of my life and perspective. Our shared history helps build on that relationship, and creating memories at Christmas, exchanging gifts, making more of life's moments, give all of us an opportunity to do that. Sharing what you've learned is a great gift.

Music has always been a part of our holiday. Mom and Dad have a record player from their first anniversary of marriage in 1961. And they still have a killer collection of vinyl. My mom and I have always made a certain Johnny Mathis recording a favorite. Mathis released dozens of albums during his career, but he only did one Christmas record with the Percy Faith Orchestra. This has my highest recommendation. Since being "at home" is what Christmas is about for me, Mathis and the Percy Faith Orchestra perform the finest version of "I'll Be Home for Christmas." The song is done with class and grace. And it makes the holiday feel good.

My professional home has been in New York City for the past twenty years. A Manhattan Christmas is one of the best anywhere: stores are decked out for the holidays, music fills the sidewalk, and restaurants are bustling with people loaded with holiday happiness. It's a great feeling. But I always come back to those childhood memories of being in a packed car driving through the streets of Cincinnati, looking for the faraway lights in anticipation of time with family.

Christmas wouldn't be Christmas without the satisfied feeling of being at home with family. It's an annual reminder of the love you share for the Christmas season, its spirit, and one another.

Bill Hemmer is the cohost of *America's Newsroom* (weekdays 9–11 a.m. ET).

Maria Bartiromo

Maria Bartiromo has fond memories of Christmases in her family's restaurant, the best Italian place in Brooklyn. Ultimately, she reminds us, family is all about always being there for one another.

I grew up in Dyker Heights, Brooklyn, a close-knit neighborhood where most of us knew everyone on the block. It was a little suburbia but close enough to New York City to give us what I learned later to be "street smarts." As a girl I played with my friends outside on the block after school. These were the kids I grew up with, after we moved to Eighty-Fourth Street when I was just a one-year-old. It was Stephanie and Anna. Johnny and Jon and Eddie. These boys and girls were my best friends. We played hopscotch and stickball and manhunt, also known as hide-and-seek. But in our game you had to get to base

Maria Bartiromo loved playing the accordion her dad bought
her as a kid–she even learned a Christmas tune or two.

first without getting tagged. My nickname on the block was "Bullet" because I was the fastest runner. They couldn't catch me at manhunt. Eddie came up with my nickname and it stuck. We'd play all day, every day, until my mom or my sister called me in for dinner. Or until we saw my dad's car turn the corner and drive down the block from work. If he was home early, we knew that could mean great news. When we saw my dad pull up early, we knew he might have pizza pies in the car for everyone on the block. My dad ran the Rex Manor restaurant, which was a few miles from our home, and the Rex had the best pizza and calzones in Brooklyn.

My grandfather built the Rex when he came to the US from Italy and settled in Brooklyn after serving in World War I. But in the 1970s, when I was growing up, my friends and I knew it as my family's restaurant and the source of my dad's awesome pizza after playing manhunt. The whole neighborhood knew my dad and the Rex. And everyone loved my dad. I am so proud of both my parents for creating this incredibly loving life for my siblings and me. They were both always so hardworking and put family first.

My grandfather Carmine Bartiromo came to this country right around 1906. He arrived in the US from Naples, Italy, with twelve dollars in his pocket. He was only thirteen years old at the time. He came over to join his father, my great-grandfather Pasquale, who had come a few years earlier and was in New York. When World War I broke out, Grandpa Carmine served in the military. He traveled to Europe once again, and after the war ended, he traveled between the US and Italy before moving here full-time and settling in Brooklyn.

I am in awe when I think about the courage my grandfather Carmine and his father, Pasquale, had to have—to leave a family and friends they knew so well, to get on a ship with a few dollars in their pockets, with only the hope and promise of opportunity in America. The dream of creating a new life for his kids and their kids. And they did exactly that. Amazing.

In Italy, Carmine was a construction worker and builder. So, after World War I ended and he settled in Brooklyn, New York, he built a restaurant—literally built it—with his cousin. They knew how to lay down bricks. They named the establishment the Rex Tavern after that famous ocean liner that transported Italians to America. Later, they changed the name to the Rex Manor because it became much more than a tavern. It was a restaurant, a catering hall, and they built a beautiful brick oven for pizza. We had two private catering rooms, a restaurant, and a big bar area, where we also served pizza.

My dad worked there his entire life, and after his service in the Korean War, he eventually took over for my grandfather in running the Rex, which became a well-known spot in Brooklyn. My whole family worked there. The only days we were closed were Mondays. That's when I would go with my dad to the Rex so he could "do the books." I would run around and slide on the floors, watching him punch numbers into a calculator. From a very young age I watched my dad manage the Rex's balance sheet. I didn't realize at the time the seeds of business acumen he was planting in me. My mom also had a full-time job at an off-track betting location. She always had a career, and I watched her become financially independent. Again, she was planting so many seeds in me for my future aspirations and confidence. My mom also helped at the Rex whenever my dad needed it. On Wednesday nights, the Rex featured "parents without partners" night. My mom would take the tickets to get in, and there was a live band. Two of my uncles were in the band. It was so ahead of its time. So I grew up in the restaurant business. And I loved every minute of working with my family. My very first job was as the coat-check girl at the Rex Manor. I still have the sign I kept on the wooden counter in the coat room. It's now framed and in my office. It reads:

Coat Check 50-cents
PLEASE PAY IN ADVANCE

During weddings and big events, most people gave me a dollar, so I was able to make great tips. And earning and saving money was such a priceless lesson.

My brother was a waiter at the Rex and my sister a hostess. Because we were also a catering hall, we hosted functions at the Rex in two private rooms. That meant we hosted a lot of parties for weddings, bar mitzvahs, anniversaries, and so on. We were a part of many families' high points and celebrations. My parents got married at the Rex; I had my Sweet Sixteen birthday party there. The Rex was a family place—not just for my own family but for the whole neighborhood. The Rex was home for the community.

Holidays at the Rex were so special. Christmastime was full of holiday parties and excitement. My dad was running the kitchen, cooking and getting his hands dirty. It was always bustling. His partner, Victor, was walking around, checking on the guests. My whole family was busy working hard and we all loved it. We worked there on Christmas Eve for part of the day, and then most years we tried to go to midnight mass at night. But first we would have our traditional fish dinner. My mom always made fish on Christmas Eve. The Feast of the Seven Fishes isn't called that in Italy and it's not an official feast day on the Roman Catholic calendar, but it was a tradition in my family. In Italy, the Christmas Eve dinner is La Vigilia (The Vigil) to commemorate the wait prior to the birth of the baby Jesus. Southern Italians, like those in my family, introduced the tradition in the US, and it goes all the way back to Little Italy in Manhattan in the late 1800s. The reason you eat fish is that in Roman Catholicism there is a rule that you abstain from eating meat prior to the celebration of any feast day like Christmas.

Like my dad, my mother was an incredible cook. And she loved doing it. She used to joke with my father that she would rather do the cooking at home because it was less work for her! He made too much of a mess. Mostly because when my dad cooked, he did it as if he were at the restaurant, with too much equipment all over. My mom would say he prepared the food as if he were cooking for the Seventh Army. Pots and pans would be heaped up on the counter, and enormous platters of whatever the two of them had cooked conquered the table. It was a lot to clean up. But it was all so loving and beautiful in our humble home. I didn't care who cooked. They were both amazing and delicious cooks.

Meanwhile, what was going on outside my home on Christmas was almost as exciting as inside. In later years, my neighborhood became iconic because of the Christmas decorations we all put up. The families in Dyker Heights took Christmas decorations very seriously. They would spend thousands of dollars on professional decorations. I mean beautiful, large Nativity sets, huge Santa Claus and reindeer sets. Music, so many lights. It was, and still is, an amazing scene! It was so well known throughout the area that people would drive from miles away to tour the streets and take in the displays of illumination and decorations. It is now referred to as "Dyker Lights."

As kids, the three of us siblings would put up all the lights on our house. We'd put displays in the bay windows in the front of the house; I always loved setting up the white lights and red- or gold-colored bows. We'd set up statues of Santa Claus outside on the grass. We loved putting up the Christmas tree together. But it was nothing compared to what my neighbors did down the block. It was something to see. Even today, people go sightseeing on my old block, causing traffic backups because they come from all over and drive at a crawl's pace down the street to take it all in.

The Rex was also beautifully decorated, but there was something about decorating the house in Dyker Heights, having the entire neighborhood out there, often at the same time, putting up their decorations that was so special. We'd walk up and down the streets throughout the neighborhood, admiring everyone's work and getting in the festive mood.

One of the other great pleasures of the season was preparing our Christmas Day meal. After we opened presents, my sister, my mother, and I would head into the kitchen. We'd get steaming pots of water boiling so that we could cook the noodles for lasagna. My mother had another large pot going in which she prepared her gravy (red sauce) for the dish. Italians refer to sauce with lots of meat in it as gravy. Like braciola, meatballs, sausage—they were all in the gravy. With onions and garlic, olive oil, fresh tomatoes, and fresh basil. We would be sampling antipasto—delicious Italian meats and cheeses, olives, peppers, sautéed mushrooms prior to that big sit-down meal—while we cooked, and spending time in the kitchen like that was, and still is, the best way to bond and be together.

My dad loves cooking with his girls. Even today, my parents come to my house and my dad and I love making a pizza together. I'll invite my sister, and my dad is in heaven cooking in my kitchen with his girls. On his amazing pizza, the most important step is to make sure the bottom of the dough cooks a little. Spread olive oil and one spoonful of tomato sauce on the rolled-out dough. Then you have to put just that in the oven for a few minutes to get the bottom hard before you take it out and start piling on toppings like mozzarella, the rest of the sauce, and grated cheese.

I thank God for my upbringing and I am so grateful that my parents put such an emphasis on family. One of the most important lessons my parents passed on was the support of family. I'll always remember a small example—I must have been a teenager and I was crying over something silly. I told my mom about it in my room one night. And I said to her, "Don't tell anyone. I'm upset." As soon as she left my room, I overheard her tell my father, my sister, then my brother. I could hear them all discussing me and why I was upset. I was furious. It was my private story and I was embarrassed. But actually, soon after, I felt better. It was such a powerful message for a kid—I understood at that moment that whatever problem I thought I had, it wasn't just my problem at all. It was my entire family's problem. And we would get through it together. I'm pretty sure that's the reason I kept shooting for the moon at school and at work. Because I knew that however it turned out, my family would support me and help me through it. That's very powerful. I am so grateful to be able to say my mother has been my best friend my entire life. And still is. And the same goes for my dad and sister and brother. I owe my family so much for their love and support. But I must say I'm a mama's girl.

My mom also taught me to become financially independent. I watched how hard my dad worked to send us to school and raise us. My mom would always encourage me to save my money, whatever little money I had to call my own. And she taught me that I had to rely on myself and that there were no shortcuts. These were very important values in our family: work hard and earn it. When I was five years old the ice cream truck came down the block and I heard the chimes. I asked my mom if I could get a cone, and she said, "You could have an ice cream cone, but how will you pay for it? Do you have any change saved?" From that moment on, I started saving all my nickels and dimes in a jar. I learned the lesson of saving at a very young age. My grandfather was a self-made man; he had my dad working at the Rex from a young age, and the same was true for my mom's family. My mom watched her mom raise four kids alone while working in a factory making women's dresses. My mom's father passed away at a young age. These values—of being a close-knit family, working hard, always doing the right thing, supporting each other, having faith in God and trust in one another—were the values I was raised on. And they were all passed down through the generations. This work ethic that I know and live comes from my grandparents. My sister and brother have passed it on to their children as well. My sister also taught her kids to follow what she called a three-part rule. Whatever money they got, whether from work or gifts, one-third of it went to savings, one-third went to charity, and they could spend the final third the way they wanted right then. It was a great lesson in earning, saving, and giving back. My mom set up savings accounts for us, and we watched them earn interest. I remember watching her set up what was called a "Christmas Club account," where you would save money every month, and around Christmas, the bank sent you a check. What a lesson. My parents grew up in the Depression. So they learned not to waste. To save everything. They knew how important it was to save because they had lived in a time of need.

Music was also a part of my upbringing. My mom forced us all to play an instrument. My sister and I both took accordion lessons. My brother played guitar. We used to take a family trip every summer, usually to the Catskill Mountains, and my mom would put us in a talent show. My mother always made sure to get me out onto the stage to sing and dance. The accordion is not the most portable of instruments. But she would push me out in front all the time regardless. My mom recently called me to let me know that she'd found my accordion in the basement. She wanted to know if I would like to have it. I told her, "Of course

I do! Who would believe that I was an accordion player? Yes." It's a beautiful instrument, and I have it on display in my living room. I did learn to play a few Christmas songs, and it's nice to have it around to serve as a reminder of all the memories I have from childhood, the Rex and how filled with the Christmas spirit that place and our home were.

Maria Bartiromo is the anchor of *Mornings with Maria* on FOX Business Network (weekdays 6–9 a.m. ET) and anchors *Sunday Morning Futures with Maria Bartiromo* (10–11 a.m. ET) on FOX News Channel.

Emily Compagno

Emily Compagno reflects on how there's a lot of joy in the things we have—but the real joy is the things that they make us remember: family, loved ones, Christmas joy.

You've likely picked a side in the fierce debate around the use of real versus artificial Christmas trees, and for those of you who know how obsessed I am with Christmas, you might be surprised by which team I'm on. Spoiler: both! But for a special reason.

My mother was diagnosed with an advanced, aggressive form of breast cancer at age thirty-five, when my two older sisters and I were all under the age of ten. We are a close-knit family and at the time lived in a small neighborhood where

Emily Compagno and her dog, Duchess.

our neighbors were part of our extended, "chosen" family. Her health crisis drew us all even closer.

At the time of my mother's diagnosis and subsequent treatment, my dad was a young US Navy physician managing her significant medical care while raising three daughters. He was stretched thin but coping as best as anyone possibly could, and we were never without love, care, and nurturing. But one Christmas, going out to buy a fresh Christmas tree just wasn't going to happen. He wasn't going to be able to buy any kind of Christmas tree.

In stepped our beloved neighbors Della and Louis Donato, whom I will forever consider surrogate grandparents. They knew my sisters and I were going to

Emily (far right) with her two older sisters and their beloved fake tree in 1990.

go through the Christmas season without a tree at our house, and they weren't about to let that happen. One day before Christmas, they knocked on the door and presented us with a tree they'd purchased: an artificial tree with *snow* on it! This California girl was absolutely mesmerized, and I was thrilled to have that magical symbol of the season in the house, covered with our traditional silver and gold tinsel, colored lights, and family ornaments. That tree was a reminder that Christmas was coming, that the Christ child would soon arrive, and that the Savior of the world's birth and all it represented would bring joy and hope to all.

In time, our prayers for my mom's recovery were answered. She won her battle with cancer. It was, and remains, our miracle. We continued to put up that artificial tree every single Christmas after that. It served as a sparkling, snowy reminder of the generosity and care other people showed to our family at a time of urgent need. Della and Louis weren't the only ones who served as guardian angels. So many other people contributed to us managing that crisis, and for every light on that tree, every ornament, we were reminded of the people who cared for us and the multiple acts of kindness and compassion we received throughout that long, difficult stretch of time. That generosity of spirit is what Christmas is all about. To this day, that tree goes up every Christmas, and it remains an enduring symbol of the faith and love that tree represented to those three little girls.

Speaking of (family) trees, my mom is a genealogist. She is a family historian and a storyteller. In our family, receiving and sending Christmas ornaments as gifts is a precious tradition. Like our artificial tree, ornaments take on special significance not because of their material value or the physicality but because of the love and stories they represent. My mom made sure we heard and knew the origins of these meaningful ornaments—who sent them, their stories, and past memories my family shared with them. And we knew exactly where to hang them: "Breakables and antiques on top, soft on the bottom." (This general rule served our house well through growing small children and cats and dogs!) Those ornaments were in part a symbolic framework for our family history—our path to the United States, our significant history of military service, and stories of our everyday lives. My mother's family is from England, Southern Germany, and Bohemia, and my father's family is Sicilian. We have ornaments that have been passed down from generation to generation, and those heirloom ornaments are special keepsakes.

Our memories are particularly important because my mother was just six years old when her beautiful mother, Olga, died of breast cancer. When my parents married, my mom's father, Hugh, gave her all their family ornaments and Nativity sets. My mom has passed along those treasures to my sisters and me, and now we all have some of those priceless heirlooms hanging from our trees in our homes. Because of this, and the stories my mother has shared with us about both sides of relatives and our history and culture, we are connected. When I look at the tree I don't just see those individual ornaments; I see all the others, the web that unites them and all of us. As meaningful as that artificial tree was in my young life, I knew I would establish my own traditions as well and couldn't wait to craft my own Christmas style. I always get a fresh Christmas tree, and I love having one in the house! The aroma, the ritual of choosing it. I'm not a Charlie Brown–style tree lover, although I do appreciate those—I get the mightiest I can fit (or carry, as was the case one year when I got one by myself as a "surprise" and had to drag that poor tree up two flights of stairs, sacrificing about ten boughs in the process)! I make sure there is individual charm and some bald spots— nothing perfect, just perfectly unique. The fresh tree has its own meaning for us, and I'm grateful my family still proudly displays the other one. We get the best of both worlds: a treasure from the past and the best of the present.

Our Italian-American heritage featured prominently in our Christmas traditions. On Christmas Eve, we got to open presents from our extended family. Most of my Sicilian family on my dad's side lived two hours away on the picturesque Monterey Peninsula, a place of rich Italian-American history. My incredible grandmother Nonnie Josephine and the memory of my grandfather Nonno Giovanni; her magical two sisters, Violet and Evelyn; her brother, Joe; my beloved uncle Nino and auntie Catherine and the best three cousins in the world; my beautiful godmother, Mary Ann; and all the rest of my wonderful family celebrated Christmas and life with us every time we were together. My dear uncle (and godfather) Sal was our close neighbor in Berkeley and would join us for our Christmas celebration. We were very close with our family, and I loved visiting them and celebrating Christmas there every year just prior to the actual holiday. At home on Christmas Day, we'd open presents from Santa and my immediate family. We were allowed to open our stockings instantly upon waking up but had to wait for everyone to be awake and downstairs to open the actual gifts. Every gift had a tag signed "From Santa" or "Love, Mom & Dad." And in every written "Mom," the *o* was a heart. Strong, rich coffee (with milk for the kids) with my dad's famous homemade Café Beaujolais coffee cake was the perfect breakfast while we exchanged gifts.

We enjoyed a huge Italian meal both nights, with stories, laughter, and talking around the table far into the night. My sisters and I took turns saying grace, and not one bite was had until we had all toasted to family and good health. *Salute!* Always we had caprese to start, presented in the *il tricolore* circular fashion with each layer of fresh, hand-sliced mozzarella cheese, fresh basil (often picked from our garden), and ripe red tomatoes encircling mixed or black olives in the center of the dish. My dad is an incredible cook, and pasta alla Siciliana or capellini with sundried tomatoes would follow, with freshly grated Parmigiano-Reggiano lightly sprinkled on top. Fresh, warm bread with olive oil for dipping and vegetables sautéed with just olive oil, lemon, and a bit of salt and pepper.

Even Emily's dog, Duchess, gets dressed up for the holidays.

Dad's Pasta alla Siciliana

¼ cup olive oil
4 cloves garlic, minced
14.5-ounce can diced or whole tomatoes
2 teaspoons dried oregano (or fresh oregano, chopped)
8–10 anchovy fillets, minced
24 Niçoise or green olives, pitted and halved
2½ tablespoons salted capers, rinsed and chopped
1 pound penne or mostaccioli

1. Bring a large pot of salted water to a boil.

2. Heat the olive oil in a large skillet over low heat. Add the garlic and sauté for 1 minute.

3. Add the tomatoes and oregano, crumbling the oregano between your fingers. Cook at a gentle simmer for 10 minutes, stirring often. If it appears dry, add a bit of water.

4. Remove from the heat and stir in the anchovies, olives, and capers.

5. Add the pasta to the boiling water and cook according to the instructions on the box until al dente. Reserve 1 cup of pasta water. Drain the pasta and return it to the pot. Add the sauce and stir to coat. Add the reserved pasta water if needed. Taste and adjust seasoning.

6. Divide among warm bowls and serve immediately.

Nonnie's Angel Hair (Capellini) Pasta with Sun-Dried Tomatoes

1 pound capellini pasta
10 ounces sun-dried tomatoes in olive oil, chopped, and oil reserved
4 cloves garlic
1 small onion, chopped
¼ cup tomato paste
1 cup dry white wine
3 tablespoons flat-leaf parsley, chopped
2 tablespoons olive oil
Crumbled goat cheese, for serving

1. Bring a large pot of salted water to a boil. Add the pasta to the boiling water and cook according to the instructions on the box until al dente. Drain the pasta, reserving 2 cups of the pasta water.

2. Add oil from the sun-dried tomatoes to a medium pan over medium-low heat and sauté the garlic and onion. Add the tomato paste, mixing continuously for 2 to 3 minutes. Add the sun-dried tomatoes and sauté. Add the wine and sauté for 10 to 15 minutes, then add the chopped parsley.

3. Mix the pasta into the sauce, stirring constantly, adding the 2 cups of reserved pasta water to moisten. Add 2 tablespoons or more of olive oil. After serving onto plates, add 2 tablespoons of goat cheese to each plate. Season with salt and pepper to taste.

My sisters and I enjoyed thimblefuls of wine alongside the adults and water with lemon slices, often from one of our lemon trees. Making our family salad was a group affair, and the dressing was always perfect, with a simple mix of olive oil and balsamic vinegar and a touch of spices. Dessert might be chilled fresh grapes in water or a light sorbet (drizzled with limoncello for the adults). We all participated, and our contributions in the kitchen and at the table in conversation were valued. All of us had jobs to help with the preparation, cooking, clearing, and dishes. And as adults, we've taken the same recipes and same traditions from a two-day celebration and turned it into a three-day one!

Our traditions and memories are also important to our family because we lived in many different places, due to my dad's military posts when we were younger and our individual paths that took us around the country later on. After many years of living in different states, my family is now blessed to all live in the Pacific Northwest. My oldest sister lives on a houseboat on Lake Union, and on December 23 we get front-row seats to Seattle's Christmas Ship Parade of Boats. This gorgeous nautical light display is a visual wonder—boats upon boats lit up with Christmas lights sail from Lake Washington through Montlake Cut to Lake Union, while the Argosy Christmas Ship blasts Christmas carols from its decorated vessel. Our family sits on the deck of the houseboat enjoying the magical parade, from tiny kayaks with glowing red Rudolph noses to stunning yachts aglow with Christmas lights and displays. We drink hot chocolate and Christmas cocktails while exclaiming over the twinkling boats and the lights reflected in the water just below our beautiful city skyline. The boat parade is a unique Christmas celebration and we are so fortunate for our equally unique way of viewing it.

On Christmas Eve, it's my turn to host the family. I look forward to this for 364 days! My Christmas obsession is definitely well represented in the decorations department, including ensuring my Doberman pinscher, Duchess, is always festive and elegant in a red ribbon or bow (or a full-blown Santa costume).

But the decorations are not overdone—there has to be a balance achieved, you see, so it's not a Christmas "explosion," but more of a generous reminder everywhere you look. Wide red silk ribbons adorn our indoor white columns like candy canes, and our long white railing beside the outside front steps gets the candy cane treatment too. Lush green garlands with white lights encircle every stair banister inside and outside, finished with large red bows. Our front door, porch, and railings get double love with garlands and extra lights, with red poinsettias, a handmade rough-wood Rudolph, a huge fresh wreath hung by a large red velvet ribbon, and lots of weather-friendly decorations welcoming visitors. I've perfected the art of decorating the outside of the house and putting up lights in the pouring rain, which seems to be an annual tradition as well.

I take my tree decorating very seriously, you guys. The ornaments (of course!) are the focal point, and they are mostly jewel tones, dominated by fuchsia and purple. Everything is sparkles, glitter, crystals, and bright and shiny. Lots of gorgeous peacocks, bells, real feathers, ballet imagery, snowflakes, and birds. My top tree skirt is a deep green that sits over a sparkly silver one—providing a perfect backdrop for my (painstakingly designed and wrapped, of course) gifts for loved ones. Quadruple strings of white lights are the secret sauce . . . and no tinsel. The tree topper? A silver glittery star, of course. Come to think of it, my house looks like a very tasteful version of the set of a TV Christmas special, minus the fake snow coming down. (Note to self: google fake-snow machines!)

As with our artificial tree during my childhood, my love for the Christmas items I've accrued over the years stems from the meaning and emotional significance behind them. Many of my decorations have been passed down through my family or gifted to me by loved ones, and it makes them even more special. A replica of Russia's Mariinsky Theatre in Saint Petersburg, where the world premiere of *The Nutcracker* ballet took place in 1892, performs seven scenes from the ballet with tiny, dancing figurines and backdrop changes, complete with a

Emily's dad, John, with his mother, Josephine, and the family nativity in 1950.

Emily's mom, Katherine, with her brother and mother, Olga, in 1953.

moving velvet stage curtain all to Pyotr Tchaikovsky's wondrous score. This is a treasured gift and quite an impressive contraption, fit for Uncle Drosselmeyer himself, and transfixes my three nieces (and me!) every time we turn it on.

Forest-green hand towels with tiny gold embroidered Christmas trees that we grew up with now hang in my powder room. My Goebel Hummel and Beatrix Potter figurine collection from my mom is my "pride and joy," as she says, and it's a love we share together. We add more to our collections each year. "More for me, then!" I crow as my sisters roll their eyes when she and I exclaim over these precious characters.

My Nativity sets are among my most special treasures. And yep, I have multiple. All of them gifts, most of them passed down through my mother and father, and each a source of delight as well as a reminder of exactly why we are celebrating this holy time. Growing up, we maintained the tradition of placing Jesus in the manger on Christmas morning, and I was thrilled when I got to be the one to place Him in the scenes. Now I maintain that same tradition, and I still hold the same reverence and excitement each time I place the tiny figurine of Him in the individual mangers. Part of my gratitude and acknowledgment comes from receiving these as family gifts—I am honored to steward these precious Nativity scenes, to care for them with the respect and honor they deserve, in order to pass them on to the next generation when the time comes. The different Nativity scenes reflect everything from the skill of woodcarving and Italian aesthetics to the whimsy and delight of Patience Brewster.

And now for the medal round: nutcrackers! These handsome gentlemen are the stars of my mantel and get a whole section of the living room to themselves. Some are handmade smokers from Oberwiesenthal of the German Erzgebirge, considered the heart of folk art and handcraft, and where my family is from. My mom brought them back from her family history travels (and given we are from there, my love of nutcrackers is clearly in my blood, and even more present in my mom, who displays hers year-round). Moreover, I began dancing ballet when I was three, and my passion for *The Nutcracker* was only enhanced by performing in it every year.

One of our family traditions was to attend the San Francisco Ballet's production of that Christmas classic every year, and we now take my three nieces to the Pacific Northwest Ballet's annual production. As an aside, the gift shop at PNB is unparalleled and simply exquisite, and many of my most impressive nutcrackers hail from there—including a commanding black glittery-and-real-feathered Drosselmeyer and a most imposing Mouse King with a jeweled velvet cape. Dance was such a significant part of my life and our family; many of our ornaments and decorations reflect our love for ballet and familiar favorites like the Swan Princess from *Swan Lake*, the Peacock from PNB's *Nutcracker*, and of course, crowns and pointe shoes galore!

Part of the magic of Christmas is spreading the spirit, good tidings and cheer. As a dancer in *The Nutcracker*, each year I performed abbreviated versions of the production in schools and elderly care facilities throughout the Bay Area. I loved performing for seniors and for children. Whether a tiny dancer performing as one of Mother Hubbard's children or a more skilled dancer performing as a snowflake, I could see how the magic of *The Nutcracker* was received by first timers and seasoned audience members alike. Now, as an adult, I appreciate having had those experiences and better understand how important it was to have a connection with those two groups in particular. We were influencing the young to develop an interest in dance and the performing arts through the magic of the timeless *Nutcracker* production. For seniors, we reignited memories from their past, showing them they weren't forgotten and expressing our gratitude for them through entertainment. As much as I loved performing, the after-show meet and greets were even better. Engaging with the kids and the seniors, connecting with them and hearing what they had to say and feeling their appreciation, was the real Christmas gift.

Years later, I was a cheerleader for the National Football League's Oakland Raiders. That was another opportunity to dance and cheer on my favorite team, but more important, we served as ambassadors to the community. Our philanthropic endeavors were extensive, but the true cheer was spreading joy throughout the community, especially with the men and women of our military. I had the honor of visiting the deployed troops in Iraq and Kuwait in 2009. Before going, I enlisted the aid of several Bay Area newspapers and radio stations to put out a call for letters and cards for the troops. The response was overwhelming and those heartfelt words and prayers meant so much to the men and women defending our country, far from home and family. One part of our performance was dedicated to reading some of the messages aloud, letting everyone share collectively in the glad tidings from home.

Hosting Christmas Eve at my house is so special for me, and I want to make it special for my family too. Everyone receives a Winter Warmer cocktail (recipe from the Ashford Castle in Ireland—apple juice, white rum, and coconut syrup, mulled with ginger, cloves, and cinnamon, and served with fresh apple and orange slices—I have carefully kept the recipe card from there for years!), and I prepare an enormous dinner, usually including cioppino. Our family holds infinite gratitude for our mom's miracle, and we are now blessed even further by my sister's three little girls, named after my Sicilian grandmother and great-aunts, who will carry on the traditions the three of us had with my mom. Both sides of my family and all of who we are is embodied in those girls. We have abundance and harmony and oh so many blessings.

Uncle Sal's Cioppino Recipe

1. Cioppino was the heart of our Christmas Eve dinner. The cioppino is by tradition made with salted codfish that has been desalted to become pliable and edible. If you cannot find salted cod, use fresh. Desalt the codfish by soaking it in a large tub of water for about forty-eight hours, changing the water two or three times.

2. Here is what I remember from seeing it being prepared: In a large heavy pot, sauté minced onion in olive oil with two bay leaves until the onion is translucent, then add minced garlic and chopped tomato, tomato sauce, and ½ cup of white wine. Simmer until it all is incorporated.

3. Then add cut-up potatoes and the desalted cod and simmer until the cod and potatoes are cooked. Add salt and pepper and a touch of crushed red pepper to give it a snap. You can add other fishes along with the cod, like snapper or even fresh tuna.

Our middle sister then hosts Christmas Day, and having that most special day with the children in their home is simply magic. Such warmth, love, and nurturing fills the home, and the day is hallmarked by joy and laughter. My sister cooks a delicious dinner with family recipes and a homemade biscotti to die for. We always stay up late sharing family stories and making new ones. It is a perfect finale to the holy holiday.

No Sicilian meal is complete without—you guessed it—vino! My dad owns and operates our family Árdíri Winery & Vineyards in the stunning Willamette Valley, Oregon, and his delicious wine is the perfect complement to our holiday meals. Knowing the wine was cultivated by my dad's effort and work, plus the added taste of family love, makes it so special to have his wine with our meals. While a practicing physician, my dad went to school at night to learn all about viticulture, and this small business is truly his labor of love. I am so proud of him. His career in pathology, specializing in DNA and polymerase chain reaction diagnostics, sparked a specialized interest into how our grapes grow. Pinot noir is genetically unstable. The double helix emblem of Árdíri is a nod to the resultant varietal diversity and differing wines produced from the original pinot stock. I love learning from him and helping out at the winery, especially in the vineyard itself and in the tasting room with our guests.

Our family gatherings at the winery include public participation, and the warmth and goodwill of our fellow neighbors maintains the Christmas spirit in full glory. Our tradition is that the day after Thanksgiving, we decorate the winery with our Christmas decorations. We laugh that although we put up the same decorations every year, somehow we are always confused by how to put up this one huge garland and struggle with it for usually about an hour, with only minimal ladder scares, before finally figuring it out. Lights adorn the property and the vineyard fencing, with multiple wreaths, garlands, and bows as finishing touches. We place candles in all the windows of our home there that stay lit all night. The tasting room is warmed by multiple roaring fires inside and out, and twinkling lights from tiny trees glow softly everywhere your eyes land.

We have spent many special Christmases at our beautiful winery, and we hold a Christmas tree lighting every year, complete with carolers, hot cocoa, and yes, lots of wine! Everyone receives a bell, and after gathering around the huge tree on the great lawn, with stars twinkling overhead and Mount Hood presiding over the horizon, everyone rings their bells together to signal the lighting of the tree. The first year we did it, we were so excited. We all rang our bells, my dad plugged in the master cord, and . . . nothing. Laughter came from the crowd, and once we got it figured out a few seconds later . . . presto! The most beautiful tree I have ever seen was lit. And the crowd roared! That remains my favorite tree lighting.

It is so special for us to see how many families have made it their tradition to hold their holiday celebrations at the winery—to provide a place where families create their own magic, fellowship, and memories is a true blessing. We are grateful for it all and are honored to share the Christmas spirit. And all the bells I have accumulated from our annual tree lightings hang on my tree at home.

I guess I should also be very grateful that I'm still around at Christmas. One of my first years in Seattle, I was executing my vision of lights everywhere but with a full crew of . . . You're Looking at Her. Trying to figure out a way to hang lights from the (peaked) second-story roofline, I climbed out of the master balcony and surveyed the canvas. Seeing the obvious danger, I was then struck by genius and fashioned an electrical cord as a "safety harness." I looped it around myself and instructed my husband to hold one end as I shimmied my way like a flat crab over the roof, carefully attaching the lights to the roofline at a glacial pace. As my husband was yelling, "THIS ISN'T SAFE! THIS ISN'T SAFE!" I was yelling, "JUST DO IT! JUST DO IT!"

It wasn't safe; I did do it. Because, Christmas.

The next year, we hired professionals to hang the lights on the outside of the house.

My parents put so much care and attention into making our Christmases, and our lives in general, so special. They put so much thought and love into how we celebrated the season. We are a family of readers, and books played a major role in our lives and at Christmas. Every night my dad read aloud to us girls with my mom listening in. Laura Ingalls Wilder's classic *Little House on the Prairie* series was a particular favorite, with my dad working his way through the series three different times. Every night he would turn to the last page we had read and begin, "As you recall . . ." In the series, one Christmas each of the Ingalls girls received a tin cup with a penny and an orange inside as their present. So my parents did the same thing for us! We each received a tin cup, a penny, and an orange—and no orange ever tasted as good.

Every year we got a very special gift from our dad: a small box of See's Bordeaux chocolates. But the special part wasn't the chocolate. Inside each box was a hand-drawn individual ticket for a trip to Yosemite National Park. The first year he did that for us, I remember thinking, "*Oh my gosh!* I got a ticket to *Yosemite!*" Yosemite National Park is one of the most beautiful spots in the country, God's gift through nature, and spending time there together every year was another present for all of us.

My family has pulled through so much and we cherish our time together. Christmas is the culmination of those emotions and lessons. We wrap ourselves up in so many traditions because we want to create a legacy for ourselves and for future generations. We understand that nothing is ever an absolute certainty but the traditions we uphold make it feel as if there are things we can count on. There were elements of the celebration of Jesus's birth that others were counting on us to incorporate. We all need that. We all need a reminder that each of our lives can be encapsulated in an ornament, a nutcracker, a cherished book. They serve as symbols of who we are and the ties that bind us together, the joy of sharing as many moments together as we can.

Those symbols are priceless. Those tiny things we do carry weight and those objects contain lifetimes. I might be seated around the table with my sisters talking about anything, when suddenly it's like I'm in a time machine. We're back in our house in the Bay Area, dancing in the bedroom together, hairbrush microphones raised to our mouths and singing along to Belinda Carlisle. Time goes so fast, but tradition and family serve as mooring posts. We don't want those decorative boats to flow past us too quickly, have them get lost in the sea of too busy, too stressed, too tired.

And we know we won't ever get too caught up that we can't laugh and appreciate the humor in situations that might otherwise have us crying.

So—and by this time this should come as no surprise—a big part of my Christmas celebration is using my Christmas-themed dishes and glassware. I start doing this immediately after Thanksgiving. Many of these Villeroy & Boch Holly and Christmas Tree dishes are ones that my mom passed down to us girls. One Christmas Eve at my home a few years ago, in order to seat everyone comfortably, someone—whose identity I shall protect—put up an additional folding table. As always, I set the table precisely and carefully: lovely tablecloth, multiple plates and dishes per setting with chargers, handmade place cards, fresh holly, a gorgeous centerpiece, sparkly candlesticks with deep-red candles, and intricately folded napkins (I have a book on napkin folding I've had since I was a child. I literally have not changed one bit).

I'm in the kitchen and suddenly I hear this noise, an odd whooshing sound I can't identify. I look at the range and the fan isn't on. What was that? Everyone freezes in the room. A nanosecond later, I hear a crash. A second crash. A third crash. Crash. Crash. Crash. CRASH. I rush out to the dining room and there on the floor, in a heap of dishes and decorations, sits my once beautifully set table at a steep angle that rivaled the *Titanic*.

That year, we ate our Christmas Eve meal on Raiders-themed paper plates. We all thought it was hysterical (and its own Christmas miracle) that me, the dancer who's also the klutz, had not been responsible for this particular calamity. We've had plenty of mishaps through the years—we still laugh about me as a young girl carrying the bowl of freshly grated Parmigiano-Reggiano to the table, only to trip and bathe the entire dining room in, as my dad phrased it, "a blanket of snow." Our first question is always "Is anyone hurt?" If not, then all is well—anything can be replaced. There's a lot of joy in the things we have, but the real joy is when they serve as reminders of family, loved ones, and Christmas joy.

I don't think we're going to make this version of crashing a Christmas party a tradition. I'm crazy about Christmas, but even I have to set some limits.

Emily Compagno currently serves as a cohost of *Outnumbered* (weekdays 12–1 p.m. ET).

Illustration Credits

Chapter 1 – Melanie Dunea

Chapter 2 – Courtesy of Jesse Watters

Chapter 3 – Courtesy of Bret Baier

Chapter 4 – Public domain

Chapter 5 – Courtesy of Lawrence Jones

Chapter 6 – Courtesy of Ainsley Earhardt

Chapter 7 – Amy Sohnen

Chapter 8 – Courtesy of John Roberts

Chapter 9 – Jill C. Smith Photography

Chapter 10 – Courtesy of Charles Payne

Chapter 11 – Courtesy of FOX News, guitar photo courtesy of John Rich

Chapter 12 – Courtesy of Martha MacCallum

Chapter 13 – Courtesy of Shannon Bream

Chapter 14 – Courtesy of Lauren Green

Chapter 15 – Courtesy of Geraldo Rivera

Chapter 16 – Courtesy of Jessica Kopecky Design

Chapter 17 – Courtesy of Janice Dean

Chapter 18 – Courtesy of Steve and Peter Doocy

Chapter 19 – Courtesy of Bill Hemmer

Chapter 20 – Monica Rich Kosann

Chapter 21 – Courtesy of Emily Compagno

About the Contributors

DANA PERINO currently coanchors the FOX News Channel morning news program *America's Newsroom* (weekdays 9–11 a.m. ET) and serves as the cohost of *The Five* (weekdays 5–6 p.m. ET). She is the host of *Dana Perino's Book Club* on FOX Nation, a streaming service that complements FOX News. She joined the network in 2009 as a contributor. From 2007 to 2009, Perino served as the White House Press Secretary under President George W. Bush.

JESSE WATTERS currently serves as the host of *Watters' World* and cohost of *The Five*. He joined FOX News Channel in 2002 as a production assistant. In 2003, Jesse made his on-camera debut, showcasing his popular man-on-the-street interviews, traveling to different locations, and quizzing individuals about politics, pop culture, and current events. He is the author of the number one *New York Times* bestseller *How I Saved the World*.

BRET BAIER currently serves as the anchor and executive editor of *Special Report with Bret Baier* (weeknights at 6–7 p.m. ET) and chief political anchor of FOX News Channel. He is also the author of four *New York Times* bestsellers, *Three Days in January: Dwight Eisenhower's Final Mission*; *Special Heart: A Journey of Faith, Hope, Courage, and Love*; *Three Days in Moscow: Ronald Reagan and the Fall of the Soviet Empire*; and his most recent book, *Three Days at the Brink: FDR's Daring Gamble to Win World War II*, which was released in October 2019.

BRIT HUME currently serves as a senior political analyst for FOX News Channel and contributes to all major political coverage on the network. He previously anchored *Special Report* and led the program for more than ten years, stepping down in December 2008. Hume joined the network in 1996.

LAWRENCE JONES currently serves as a *FOX & Friends* Enterprise Reporter. He joined FOX News Channel in December 2018. Jones frequently appears on *Outnumbered*, fills in as a guest cohost on *The Five*, and has helmed FNC's 7 p.m. ET program *FOX News Primetime*. He also provides commentary and analysis across both FNC and FOX Business Network daytime and primetime programming.

AINSLEY EARHARDT is the cohost of *FOX & Friends* (weekdays 6–9 a.m. ET) alongside Steve Doocy and Brian Kilmeade. She joined the FOX News Channel in 2007 and is based in New York. In addition to her role on *FOX & Friends*, Earhardt is host of FOX Nation's *Ainsley's Bible Study*.

BRIAN KILMEADE is the cohost of *FOX & Friends* (weekdays 6–9 a.m. ET) alongside Steve Doocy and Ainsley Earhardt. Kilmeade is also the host of the *Brian Kilmeade Show* on FOX News Radio and is the author of several books: *Sam Houston and the Alamo Avengers: The Texas Victory that Changed American History*; *Andrew Jackson and the Miracle of New Orleans: The Battle that Shaped America's Destiny*; and *New York Times* bestsellers *The Games Do Count: America's Best and Brightest on the Power of Sports*; *It's How You Play the Game: The Powerful Sports Moments that Taught Lasting Values to America's Finest*; and *George Washington's Secret Six: The Spy Ring that Saved the American Revolution*.

JOHN ROBERTS currently serves as the coanchor of *America Reports* (weekdays 1–3 p.m. ET) on FOX News Channel. He previously served as the Chief White House correspondent for four years during the Trump Administration. Roberts joined the network as a senior national correspondent in January 2011, based in the Atlanta bureau. Over the course of his career, Roberts has been a recipient of several awards, including a local Emmy, a New York Press Club Award, and three national Emmy Awards for his coverage of the Atlanta Olympic bombing, the death of Princess Diana, and the TWA crash. In 2006, he received an Edward R. Murrow Award for his coverage of the war in Israel.

SANDRA SMITH serves as the coanchor of *America Reports* (weekdays 1–3 p.m. ET) on FOX News Channel. She joined the company in October 2007 as a reporter for FOX Business Network. On *America Reports*, Smith and coanchor John Roberts are joined by newsmakers and experts to discuss the latest afternoon headlines and issues of the day. Previously, Smith served as the coanchor of morning news program *America's Newsroom* (weekdays 9–11 a.m. ET) and *Outnumbered* (weekdays 12–1 p.m. ET) alongside coanchor Harris Faulkner and rotating panelists.

CHARLES PAYNE is the host of *Making Money with Charles Payne* (weekdays 2–3 p.m. ET) on FOX Business Network. He joined FBN in October 2007 as a contributor and is also a contributor to FOX News Channel, frequently appearing on shows such as *Your World with Neil Cavuto* and *FOX & Friends*. He began his career on Wall Street as an analyst at EF Hutton in 1985.

JOHN RICH is the host of *The Pursuit! with John Rich* on FOX Nation, as well as a country music singer and songwriter. He's one half of the duo Big & Rich and is a multiple Grammy nominee. All of Big & Rich's albums have made the country top ten, including their country chart-topping 2004 debut, *Horse of a Different Color.*

MARTHA MACCALLUM currently serves as the anchor and executive editor of *The Story with Martha MacCallum* (weekdays 3–4 p.m. ET). She joined FOX News Channel in January 2004 and is based in New York. In 1997 and 2003, MacCallum was the recipient of the American Women in Radio and Television award for her reporting. She is the author of the *New York Times* bestseller *Unknown Valor.*

SHANNON BREAM currently serves as the anchor of *FOX News @ Night with Shannon Bream* (weekdays 12–1 a.m. ET). She joined the network in 2007 as a Washington, DC–based correspondent covering the Supreme Court. In addition to her role as anchor, Bream is a chief legal correspondent for the network and the host of *Livin' the Bream*, a podcast on FOX News Radio. Most recently, Bream authored FOX News Books' number one *New York Times* bestseller *The Women of the Bible Speak: The Wisdom of 16 Women and Their Lessons for Today.*

LAUREN GREEN currently serves as FOX News Channel's chief religion correspondent based in the New York bureau. She joined FNC in 1996. Green reported live from Rome in 2013 on the election of Pope Francis, as well as on the retirement of Pope Benedict XVI. She also provided live coverage of the beatification of Pope John Paul II from Rome in 2011 and Pope Benedict XVI's visit to the United States in 2008.

GERALDO RIVERA currently serves as a roaming correspondent at large for FOX News Channel. He joined the network in 2001 as a war correspondent. Rivera has received more than 170 awards for journalism, including the prestigious George Foster Peabody Award, three national and seven local Emmys, two duPont-Columbia Awards, and two Scripps Howard Awards.

RACHEL CAMPOS-DUFFY serves as a cohost of *FOX & Friends Weekend*. In addition, Campos-Duffy is the host of *Moms* on FOX Nation. The program aims to shine a light on family life and motherhood with women from across the country. She is also a recurring guest host on the network's hit shows *FOX & Friends* and *Outnumbered*. She is married to former congressman and FOX News Media contributor Sean Duffy. They have nine children.

SEAN DUFFY serves as a FOX News Media contributor, providing political analysis across all FOX News Media platforms. For nearly nine years, Duffy represented the people of Wisconsin's Seventh Congressional District, the state's largest district. While in Congress, he served on the Financial Services Committee and as the chairman of the Subcommittee on Housing, Community Development and Insurance. He is married to *FOX and Friends Weekend* cohost Rachel Campos-Duffy.

JANICE DEAN currently serves as the senior meteorologist for FOX News Channel. In addition, she is the morning meteorologist for *FOX & Friends* (weekdays 6–9 a.m. ET). She joined the network in January 2004. Janice is also the author of *Make Your Own Sunshine* and the *New York Times* bestseller *Mostly Sunny*.

STEVE DOOCY currently serves as the cohost of FOX News Channel's *FOX & Friends* (weekdays 6–9 a.m. ET). He is the number one *New York Times* bestselling author, with his wife, Kathy, of *The Happy in a Hurry Cookbook* and *The Happy Cookbook*. Steve is the proud father of three, including FOX News White House correspondent Peter Doocy.

PETER DOOCY currently serves as a White House correspondent for FOX News Channel. He joined the network in 2009 as a general assignment reporter based in the New York bureau. In this position, Doocy covers the president of the United States' domestic and international activities as well as the issues impacting the administration.

BILL HEMMER is the cohost of *America's Newsroom* (weekdays 9–11 a.m. ET). As one of the network's top breaking-news anchors, Hemmer has provided extensive live coverage of several major stories throughout his fifteen-plus years at FNC, including every election cycle since joining the network.

MARIA BARTIROMO is the anchor of *Mornings with Maria* on FOX Business Network (weekdays 6–9 a.m. ET) and anchors *Sunday Morning Futures with Maria Bartiromo*, the most watched Sunday-morning program on cable (10 a.m. ET) on FOX News Channel. She joined FBN as global markets editor in January 2014.

EMILY COMPAGNO currently serves as the cohost of *Outnumbered* on FOX News Channel. Compagno holds a bachelor of arts in political science from the University of Washington, where she was awarded the US Air Force Reserve Officer Training Corps' Cadet of the Quarter Award. She holds her juris doctor from the University of San Francisco School of Law, where she was president of the Federalist Society and articles editor of the *Intellectual Property Law Bulletin*.